Table of Contents

W9-BCQ-826

About the Authors

Helga Schmitz

Helga is a native of Germany and has lived in the United States for the past 25 years. She has taught all levels of German from elementary school through college. For the past 20 years, Helga has been the Foreign Language Coordinator and a German teacher at Overland High School in the Cherry Creek School District in Aurora, Colorado. Helga is a consultant for EMC/Paradigm Publishing and translates teaching materials for Blaine Ray. As a result of attending Blaine Ray's workshops, Helga changed her philosophy on teaching foreign languages. Since then she has made TPRS the focal point in her classroom instruction.

Melanie Polito

A native of Chicago, Illinois, Melanie attended the University of Colorado at Boulder where she received a double major in Germanic Studies and Spanish along with her secondary teaching certificate. Melanie became acquainted with TPRS at Blaine Ray's workshops. She then applied the method in her classroom, where she immediately saw the benefits in her students' improved language performance. She currently teaches Spanish and German at Overland High School in the Cherry Creek School District in Aurora, Colorado, and uses the TPRS method exclusively.

Helga Schmitz and Melanie Polito have been developing curriculum and providing in-service training for teachers on the TPRS approach for the past few years.

TPR Storytelling Manual

Helga Schmitz
Melanie Polito

EMCParadigm Publishing
Saint Paul, Minnesota

. runston

Editors
Alejandro Vargas Bonilla
Belia Jiménez Lorente

Illustrator
Hetty Mitchell

Acknowledgments

We would like to thank the Cherry Creek School District and our superintendent, Dr. Monte Moses, for their encouragement. We would also like to recognize the Overland High School administration and our principal, Mr. John Buckner, for their support. Finally, special thanks go to our students for their honest feedback.

Helga Schmitz and Melanie Polito

ISBN 0-8219-2806-6

Published by EMC/Paradigm Publishing
875 Montreal Way
St. Paul, Minnesota 55102
800-328-1452
www.emcp.com
E-mail: educate@emcp.com

Printed in the United States of America
5 6 7 8 9 10 XXX 09 08 07 05

Introduction

Background of TPR Storytelling

Dr. James Ascher's Total Physical Response approach (TPR) teaches language through commands. In 1990 Blaine Ray took TPR one step further and added a storytelling component, creating Total Physical Response Storytelling (TPRS). This method is based on Dr. Stephen Krashen's research on second language acquisition strategies. With the addition of storytelling, Ray found that students could learn a wider range of vocabulary and grammar. In TPRS teachers begin by preteaching new vocabulary through gestures, then using this vocabulary in mini-situations and finally incorporating it into telling and acting out a story.

This TPRS manual presents Spanish vocabulary and grammar based on the corresponding chapters of *Navegando 1*. Teachers may choose between two ways of beginning to teach with TPRS.

1. Teachers may prefer to begin with classical TPR and then continue with TPRS. For suggestions on starting with classical TPR, refer to the list of classical TPR vocabulary and the classical TPR sample lesson on pages 81-85 at the end of this manual. (A list of resources appears on page 98 for further information on the classical TPR approach.)
2. Teachers may choose to begin immediately with *Capítulo 1* of this manual.

Pedagogical Considerations

The TPRS approach to foreign language learning constitutes a change in how students develop language proficiency. TPRS is a highly interactive style of teaching that focuses on the language skills of listening and speaking while also addressing writing, reading and cultural understanding. Students' diverse learning styles and the multiple intelligences are honored as well. In the TPRS approach to achieving language proficiency there are three main components: low affective filter, comprehensible input and acquisition.

Low Affective Filter

An important component of the TPRS teaching process is a classroom environment with a low affective filter. According to Stephen Krashen, the affective filter is a mental block caused by factors such as high anxiety, lack of confidence, low motivation and being on the defensive. Krashen contends that the affective filter is the lowest during childhood and rises dramatically at around puberty, a time considered a turning point in language acquisition.

In a classroom with a low affective filter, students are genuinely involved in a language-rich environment, to the point that they forget they are interacting with a foreign language. In using TPRS materials, students focus on learning the story line as opposed to the structure of the second language. Teachers should not force speech beyond students' acquisition level and should avoid making frequent corrections. These negative factors raise the affective filter and prevent input from reaching the language acquisition device. In a classroom environment with a low affective filter, students are highly motivated, have a high level of self-esteem and a low level of concern.

Comprehensible Input

The main component of the development of second language skills is comprehensible input. Comprehensible input involves messages that language learners are able to understand. Krashen says that real language production takes place only after students have built up competence via input. A language-rich environment that offers extensive comprehensible input provides a foundation for natural language acquisition.

The step-by-step process of teaching with TPRS that is explained in this manual provides comprehensible input in a variety of ways:

1. Teachers present new vocabulary words and expressions by associating them with gestures (TPR).
2. Teachers act out the mini-situations as they narrate them.
3. Teachers point to the illustrations in the manual while telling the basic story.

Acquisition vs. Learning

This TPRS manual focuses on students' acquisition of language. Language acquisition (as opposed to language learning) is the end product when teachers establish a classroom environment based on a low affective filter and then provide authentic, language-rich comprehensible input. A child learns his or her native language in a similar manner. The child receives consistent encouragement from his or her environment because it offers a low affective filter. The child is also surrounded by plenty of comprehensible input. These factors result in the child's language acquisition.

Acquisition is an effortless, involuntary process which results in long-term memory. Acquisition takes place when students focus on the message (idea) and not on the form of the message (grammar). It is a holistic process that involves the right hemisphere of the brain. When students can produce language without having to consider a rule but just by knowing that it sounds right, that's when language acquisition has taken place.

On the other hand, language learning is an analytical process that occurs in the left hemisphere of the brain. Learning leads to short-term language retention. In a language learning environment students often concentrate on repeating, memorizing and studying grammar rules and verb conjugations. The focus is on how the message is expressed rather than on the message itself. Language learning requires premature accuracy that results in a high affective filter, low self-esteem and therefore minimal language production.

Frequently-asked Questions about TPRS

Can I teach with TPRS if my colleagues are not using it or if my administration is not supportive?

Yes. Most likely you will need to follow your district's curriculum. You will probably need to give specified standardized tests. Demonstrate to your principal that you will be meeting your curricular goals by teaching with TPRS. Also set up a small pilot program in which you compare a TPRS class

and a control group (traditional class). Document your students' progress throughout the year and share the results with other teachers and the administration. Finally, always keep the lines of communication open between yourself and the administration.

How will my students perform on standardized tests?

According to Blaine Ray, students in TPRS classes who take national standardized tests consistently score better than the national average. In addition, the number of students of all ability levels who continue with the same foreign language continues to rise.

Do I have to start teaching with TPRS at the beginning of the school year?

No. You may begin the process at any time. First try out one chapter, then assess students' progress and finally ask students for their feedback.

How is grammar taught in the TPRS classroom?

When students make a grammatical error in speaking, teachers may choose to say the sentence again correctly. However, students should be corrected minimally so as not to interfere with communication. As was previously mentioned, one of the goals in the TPRS classroom is to lower the affective filter. The more teachers emphasize correctness, the more hesitant students will be to speak. Since teachers speak with grammatical accuracy, students will get used to hearing correct language and will imitate it. Oral grammatical accuracy will occur with increased use of the language and with extensive comprehensible input.

Grammar can be incorporated into written work by having students rewrite the basic story from a different perspective. For example, they can change the story's focus from the third person singular to the first person. According to Krashen, conscious application of grammar in writing is permissible since it does not inhibit communication. When grammar-related questions spontaneously arise in class, take several minutes to explain the concept briefly.

How does TPRS impact the pace of the curriculum?

Expect the pace to be somewhat slower than in a traditional class, since acquiring language through telling stories takes more time than learning the rules of the language. However, the pace picks up as students and teachers become more familiar with the process. As students' vocabularies increase and they experience long-term retention, less time is necessary to review previously taught material. Therefore, in the final analysis, teaching using TPRS saves time.

What can students in the TPRS classroom do when there is a substitute teacher?

Remember that students are already familiar with the TPRS process. If the classroom teacher has already introduced the new vocabulary in the chapter, students may draw pictures to accompany the new words. If the teacher has finished presenting the basic story, students may invent a new ending or add on to the story. Students could also work together in teams to compose their own story using previously learned vocabulary.

Is TPRS only for energetic teachers?

In beginning to teach with TPRS, it is true that teachers expend more energy than usual to offer students enough comprehensible input to be successful learners. Teachers strive to create a positive attitude toward learning a foreign language and to build students' confidence as they use it. Seeing students' enthusiasm about coming to class and learning the language through stories tends to energize teachers. The key is to achieve a successful balance between time when teachers demonstrate the language and time when students practice it. As teachers become more experienced with TPRS, they build in activities, such as partner work, to alleviate some of the physical demands of the job. For example, students can illustrate vocabulary and basic stories. They can also work in groups to practice, present and invent stories.

In TPRS classes, there are not a lot of written homework assignments or tests, so teachers have less paperwork. Since TPRS language teaching takes place predominantly in the classroom, teachers have more available planning time.

How can we integrate students who transfer from a traditional class into a TPRS classroom?

Students from traditional classes enter the TPRS classroom expecting that their language production will be excessively monitored. These students need an explanation of the differences between a traditional and a TPRS class. Teachers need to ease new students into the TPRS process by allowing them to observe the new approach and by giving them a sufficient silent period in order to raise their comfort level. Hopefully, the affective filter will gradually decrease and these students will gain confidence in their language ability.

Chapter Organization

Each chapter in this manual has the same format and design for easy identification and reference. There are two stories in each chapter, a Basic Story and an Advanced Story. The Basic Story focuses on new vocabulary that is introduced in the corresponding chapter of *Navegando 1* and includes easily recognizable cognates. The Advanced Story contains more new vocabulary from the chapter, cognates and additional vocabulary that has not yet been presented in the corresponding textbook chapter. These additional words are listed in the Additional Vocabulary. Teachers can present the Basic Story, the Advanced Story or both, depending on their familiarity with TPRS, their students' enthusiasm and time considerations. The following sections are included in each chapter:

Basic Story

Step 1 (Gesturing New Vocabulary) outlines a 12-step approach to introducing and practicing the new words and expressions in the upcoming story. This new vocabulary is listed in the Spanish column, the English equivalent is given in the English column and a possible gesture for each word or expression is offered in the Gesture column. Note that the indicated gestures serve only as suggestions. Teachers may want to use their own ideas and imagination in presenting these words and expressions to their students. The vocabulary is listed in the same sequence in which it appears in bold type in the Basic Story. Teachers learn how to gesture each new word as well as how to present, practice, check comprehension (using sample questions), review and quiz this new vocabulary. For teachers' convenience, this Spanish vocabulary list is reproduced in larger type in the Appendix. Teachers can use these sheets as blackline masters to make overhead transparencies or individual student copies.

Step 2 (Presenting the Situations) lists suggestions on how to teach the new vocabulary words in the context of a short narrative (Situation) that often includes conversational exchanges. There are three Situations that precede each Basic Story.

Step 3 (Teaching the Basic Story). At the bottom of the second page is the Basic Story, the "heart" of the chapter and the suggested text, that accompanies the illustrations on the third page. Having learned the basic vocabulary and applied it in context in the Situations, students are now ready to use what they have learned to retell the Basic Story using visual cues and guide words. The fourth page offers 13 suggestions on how to teach the Basic Story, some of which include Yes/No Questions, Comprehension Questions and a Changed Story for students to correct. Several ideas for assessment focus on evaluating orally how much language students have acquired.

Advanced Story

The Advanced Story follows the same format and design as the Basic Story. Teachers may choose to use this story to reinforce the vocabulary presented earlier or to challenge students beyond the Basic Story. The Advanced Story contains more new vocabulary, cognates and additional words that have not yet been presented in the corresponding textbook chapter. These new words are listed in the Additional Vocabulary in order of their presentation, as are any new words that appear in the Situations. Teachers may want to use their own ideas in gesturing this additional vocabulary.

Appendix

Following the last chapter is an Appendix with the following sections:

High-frequency TPR Vocabulary — a list of the informal command forms of common Spanish verbs, their English equivalents and a suggested gesture for each one. Teaching vocabulary by means of TPR improves listening comprehension, aids long-term memory and uses body movement extensively before and after speaking. These command forms can be used throughout the TPRS process to make the learning experience highly interactive and enjoyable. Also included are lists of common adverbs, adjectives, body parts, colors and classroom objects.

Sample TPR Lesson — a step-by-step model to show how the words in the High-frequency TPR Vocabulary can be taught to students. It consists of a short vocabulary list of selected words and expressions from the High-frequency TPR Vocabulary, nine steps to follow in teaching them, a narrative in which these words are used in context and several extension activities. Teachers may want to use this sample lesson before they start teaching the Basic and Advanced Stories in this manual. Another option is to use this lesson as the first in a series of lessons to teach all or part of the High-frequency TPR Vocabulary.

Basic and Advanced Story Vocabulary — a list of the new Spanish words and expressions that have been introduced in the Basic and Advanced Stories of each chapter. Each list appears here in larger type so that teachers can use these sheets as blackline masters to make overhead transparencies or individual student copies.

Assessment Rubric — a tool to use in evaluating how much language has been acquired and to what degree.

Bibliography — a list of suggested references that deal with both TPR and TPRS.

Step-by-step Approach to Teaching with TPRS

The Basic and Advanced Stories are taught using the three-step approach:

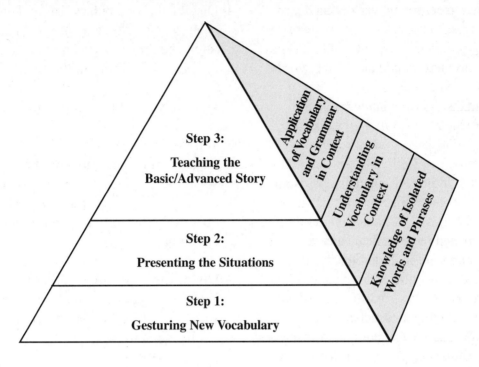

In the following section each of the three steps is described in detail. Throughout this manual, the steps and accompanying procedures are shown in abbreviated form in the left-hand column to constantly remind teachers of the process. Follow these steps as outlined in order to ensure students' success.

Step 1: Gesturing New Vocabulary

Purpose: To introduce the new vocabulary.

The vocabulary lists for the Basic and Advanced Stories come from the vocabulary found in the corresponding chapter of *Navegando 1*. Presenting new words and expressions by using gestures allows for a silent period in which students are not required to speak before they are ready. The process also involves them kinesthetically as well as visually and promotes long-term retention. This step is the foundation of vocabulary acquisition.

1. Show the vocabulary list on the right, covering up the English and Gesture columns. You may choose to make an overhead transparency of it, using the larger-print

blackline master in the Appendix. Note that words and expressions are listed in the order in which they appear in the Basic/Advanced Story. Verbs are listed in the conjugated form that appears in the story. Once a verb is listed in the vocabulary section, other forms of it may be used in stories and situations.

2. Introduce the first three words/expressions.

3. Say the words one at a time and do the gestures. Students associate the gestures with the vocabulary. When gesturing the verbs, be sure to teach the verb's subject as well. For example, if the subject is "I," students point to themselves and then gesture the verb.

4. Have students imitate the gestures silently. Make sure that all students perform the gestures. Do not allow students to ask for or give the English equivalents of the new words at this point.

5. Say the words and have students gesture with their eyes closed.

6. Test individual students randomly. Say a word and have students do the gesture. (If a word is not understood by several students, it must be included when teaching the following set of words.)

7. Do gestures and have students say the words.

8. Say the words and have students give the English equivalents.

9. Repeat this process (Steps 1-8) for the next set of three words until the vocabulary list is all presented.

10. Ask questions and have students answer. Sample questions are included for each story, and teachers are encouraged to expand on them. Teachers can also give students novel commands for additional practice and to add interest to the class. Novel commands use the targeted vocabulary in a sentence with a novel meaning. For example, if the verb "walk" is being taught, say "Walk on your hands!", "Walk in a circle!" or "Walk hand in hand with (*name of student*)!"

11. The following day review the vocabulary list using the above steps with increased speed.

12. You may also want to check students' comprehension by creating matching quizzes and fill-in-the-blank exercises. These quizzes may be unannounced in order to assess how well students have acquired the new vocabulary.

Note: Some ways to invent gestures include referencing American Sign Language books, making them up or soliciting student input.

Step 2: Presenting the Situations

Purpose: To apply the new vocabulary words in a believable context.

There are three situations for each Basic/Advanced Story. In these situations, all words and expressions in the preceding vocabulary list are used at least once in context.

1. Display the vocabulary list on the preceding page in class. Students use the list as a reference. You may want to make a copy of the blackline master in the Appendix.

2. Pick student actors for the first situation.

3. Tell the first situation in an animated way. At the same time help student actors perform the situation. To give students a visual clue to help them remember the situation, place people and objects consistently in specific places in the classroom.

4. Divide the class into small groups. Repeat the situation as each group performs it simultaneously. An option is for teachers to tell the situation and students to draw it.

5. Repeat Steps 2-4 for the remaining situations.

Step 3: Teaching the Basic/Advanced Story

Purpose: To use the vocabulary to tell a story.

Initially, the objective is for students to understand what happens in the story. The end goal, after following the first ten steps listed below, is for students to produce the story actively. The words in the vocabulary list appear sequentially in bold type in the story. The Basic Story focuses on words and expressions that are introduced in the corresponding chapter of *Navegando 1* along with easily recognizable cognates. The Advanced Story includes additional vocabulary from the chapter, cognates and other related vocabulary that has not yet been presented in the corresponding textbook chapter. Teachers may want to use their own ideas in gesturing the additional vocabulary in the Advanced Story and Situations. Grammar items that students have not yet encountered in the corresponding textbook chapters may appear in the stories. For example, students may learn in context direct and indirect object pronouns, reflexive verbs, the subjunctive, etc.

Three basic elements in most TPRS stories motivate students and make their learning experience more fun:

Bizarre situations — TPRS stories are not "normal." For example, in these stories students don't go home, but they might go instead to the moon, Death Valley or Timbuktu.

Exaggeration — Stories use adjectives like "best," "prettiest" and "little" as well as unrealistically large numbers, quantities and sizes.

Personalization — Teachers should use their students' names wherever names occur in situations and stories. Also substitute the names of places and events in your city/town if possible. Stories are more interesting to students if they touch on activities that they commonly do. Personalized, reality-based narratives are also easier for students to remember.

1. Display the vocabulary list (on the first page of the story) in class. Students use the list as a reference. You may want to make a copy of the blackline master in the Appendix.

2. Show illustrations (on the third page of the story), then tell the story. Have students follow along.

3. Pick student actors for the story.

4. Tell the story in an animated way. At the same time help student actors perform the story. To give students a visual clue to help them remember the story, place people and objects consistently in specific places in the classroom.

5. Ask Yes/No Questions. Sample questions are included for each story, and teachers are encouraged to expand on them.

6. Ask Comprehension Questions about the story. Sample questions are included for each story, and teachers are encouraged to expand on them.

7. Read the Changed Story and have students correct it. Sample substitutions are included for each story, and teachers are encouraged to expand on them.

8. Collaborate with students in establishing a list of guide words and then display the list. Note: Guide words are a brief list of difficult words or phrases that occur in the story. They do not include words from the story's vocabulary list. Guide words have been previously taught, but now they are used in a different context and students may no longer remember them. The purpose of guide words is to prevent students from regressing to more basic vocabulary and grammar. For example, even though the past tense is used in a certain chapter, students may regress to the use of the present tense unless a guide word can offer a meaningful clue.

9. Have students practice with partners using only the story's illustrations (on the third page of the story) and the guide words (if needed). The pictures help students remember the story without memorizing it.

10. Have volunteers tell the story to the class. Students may use illustrations and guide words, if necessary.

11. Assessment: Have students record the story on audiocassettes. Students may use only the illustrations. Guide words may be used by students who need more direction. Evaluate the cassettes and include them in students' portfolios. Teachers may want to use the Assessment Rubric in the Appendix to evaluate how much language students have acquired and to what degree.

12. Collaborate with students in writing the story based on the illustrations. Write the story as students copy it.

13. Have partners invent a new story or alter the original story. Have them draw new or altered illustrations and then tell the story to the class.

CAPÍTULO 1

	Spanish	English	Gesture

**Basic
Story**

Step 1 | Gesturing New Vocabulary

Purpose: To introduce the new vocabulary.

1. Show the vocabulary list on the right, covering up the English and Gesture columns.

2. Introduce the first three words/ expressions.

3. Say the words one at a time and do the gestures.

4. Have students imitate the gestures silently.

5. Say the words and have students gesture with their eyes closed.

6. Test individual students randomly. Say a word and have students do the gesture. (If a word is not understood by several students, it must be included when teaching the following set of words.)

7. Do gestures and have students say the words.

8. Say the words and have students give the English equivalents.

9. Repeat this process (Steps 1-8) for the next set of three words until the vocabulary list is all presented.

10. Ask questions and have students answer.

   Sample Questions:
   ¿Cómo te llamas?
   ¿Cuántos años tienes?
   ¿De dónde eres?
   ¿Qué hora es?
   *¿Hablas mucho con
      muchachos/muchachas?*

11. The following day review the vocabulary list using the above steps with increased speed.

12. You may also want to check students' comprehension by creating matching quizzes and fill-in-the-blank exercises.

Note: Some ways to invent gestures include referencing American Sign Language books, making them up or soliciting student input.

Spanish	English	Gesture
(él) tiene	(he) has	Bring both hands toward your chest.
Son las nueve y media.	It is 9:30.	Demonstrate time on a clock.
buenos días	good day	Wave.
(ella) dice	(she) says	Point hand toward your mouth.
(él) mira	(he) looks	Place a hand horizontal to ground above your eyes.
la muchacha	girl	Point to a girl.
(yo) quiero	(I) want	Gesture "*Quiero....*"
hablar	to talk	Mimic talking.
¿Qué hora es?	What time is it?	Shrug your shoulders and point to a watch.
Son las diez menos veinte.	It is 9:40.	Demonstrate time on a clock.
(él) escribe	(he) writes	Write in your palm.
¡Hasta mañana!/¡Hasta luego!	See you tomorrow!	Wave good-bye.
me llamo	my name is	Point to yourself and say your name.
¿Cómo te llamas?	What's your name?	Say *Me llamo* (name). Point to a student and say *¿Cómo te llamas?*
Mucho gusto.	Nice to meet you.	Shake hands.
¿Cuántos años tienes?	How old are you?	Say *Tengo* (number) *años.* Point to a student and say *¿Cuántos años tienes?*
Tengo catorce años.	I am 14.	Give an age.
¿De dónde eres?	Where are you from?	Shrug your shoulders. Point to a map.
Soy de Guatemala.	I am from Guatemala.	Point to a map.
Gracias.	Thank you.	Nod.
de nada	you're welcome	Say *Gracias.* Person says *De nada.*

Purpose: To apply new vocabulary words in a believable context.

1. Display the vocabulary list (page 1) in class. Students use the list as a reference.

2. Pick student actors for the first situation.

3. Tell the first situation in an animated way. At the same time help student actors perform the situation.

4. Divide the class into small groups. Repeat the situation as each group performs it simultaneously.

5. Repeat Steps 2-4 for the remaining situations.

Situations

1 Felipe está en el parque y **tiene** su pelota de básquetbol. (*Famous basketball player*) **mira** a Felipe y le **dice** "**¿Cómo te llamas**?" "**Me llamo** Felipe" le dice él nerviosamente. "¡Eres mi héroe!" (*Famous basketball player*) le dice "**Mucho gusto. ¿Cuántos años tienes**?" Felipe responde "**Tengo catorce años**. Por favor, **escribe** tu nombre en la pelota de básquetbol". "Sí." "**Gracias**." "**De nada**" le dice (*famous basketball player*).

2 Carlos está en (*department store*). Carlos **quiere** un CD de (*popular band*) y mira los CDs. Una **muchacha** le dice "¡Hola!" Él le dice "**¡Buenos días**!" "**¿Qué hora es**?" "**Son las diez menos veinte**." "¡Ay caramba!" dice la muchacha. "¡Perdón! Solamente **son las nueve y media**." "Gracias. **¡Hasta luego**!"

3 Susana mira a una muchacha nueva en la clase de matemáticas que no **habla** inglés. Habla solamente español con otra muchacha. Susana le dice "**¿De dónde eres**?" Ella dice "**Soy de Guatemala**". "¡Qué interesante! **¡Hasta mañana**!"

Basic Story

El primer día

José **tiene** seis clases. **Son las nueve y media** y está en la clase de español. "**¡Buenos días**, clase!" **dice** la Señora Rodríguez. José **mira** a **la muchacha** nueva en la clase. Mira y mira y mira a la muchacha. "**¡Quiero hablar** con la muchacha nueva! ¿Qué hora es? (*José thinks to himself.*) ¡Ay! **¡Son las diez menos veinte**!" José **escribe** un poema romántico a la muchacha nueva. "¿Qué hora es? ¡Excelente! Son las diez y cuarto!" La señora Rodríguez le dice a José "**¡Hasta mañana**!" José le dice "**¡Hasta luego**!" José le dice a la muchacha "¡Hola! **Me llamo** José. **¿Cómo te llamas**?" La muchacha le dice "Me llamo Josefina". "**Mucho gusto**, Josefina" dice él. "**¿Cuántos años tienes**?" "**Tengo catorce años**" dice ella. "**¿De dónde eres**?" dice el muchacho. "**Soy de Guatemala**" dice la muchacha. "Tengo un poema para ti." (*He gives her the poem.*) "¡Hasta luego! Tengo clase." "**Gracias**" dice Josefina. "**De nada**. ¡Hasta luego!" dice José. "Hasta mañana" dice Josefina.

Purpose: To use the vocabulary to tell a story.

1. Display the vocabulary list (page 1) in class. Students use the list as a reference.
2. Show illustrations (page 3), then tell the story. Have students follow along.
3. Pick student actors for the story.
4. Tell the story in an animated way. At the same time help student actors perform the story.
5. Ask **Yes/No Questions**.

> ¿Tiene José la clase de matemáticas a las nueve y media? (no)
> ¿Quiere hablar José con la muchacha nueva? (sí)
> ¿Se llama Josefina la muchacha nueva? (sí)
> ¿Tiene la muchacha quince años? (no)
> ¿Es Josefina de Cuba? (no)

6. Ask **Comprehension Questions** about the story.

¿A quién mira José?	José mira a una muchacha nueva de la clase.
¿Qué escribe José?	Él escribe un poema romántico.
¿Cuántos años tiene Josefina?	Josefina tiene catorce años.
¿De dónde es Josefina?	Es de Guatemala.
José escribe un poema. ¿Qué dice Josefina?	Gracias.

7. Read the **Changed Story** and have students correct it.

> José tiene seis clases. Son las (1) <u>tres menos diez</u> y está en la clase de español. "¡Buenos días, clase!" dice la Señora Rodríguez. José mira a la muchacha nueva de la clase. Mira y mira y mira a la muchacha. "¡Quiero hablar con la muchacha nueva! ¿Qué hora es? (*José thinks to himself.*) ¡Ay! ¡Son las diez menos veinte!" José escribe un poema romántico a la muchacha nueva. (2) "<u>¿Cuántos años tiene ella</u>? ¡Excelente! Son las diez y cuarto!" La señora Rodríguez le dice a José "¡Hasta mañana!" José le dice "¡Hasta luego!" José le dice a la muchacha "¡Hola! (3) <u>Hasta luego</u>. ¿Cómo te llamas?" La muchacha le dice "Me llamo Josefina". "Mucho gusto, Josefina" dice él. "¿Cuántos años tienes?" "Tengo catorce años" dice ella. (4) "<u>¿Qué hora es</u>?" dice el muchacho. "Soy de Guatemala" dice la muchacha. "Tengo un poema para ti." (*He gives her the poem.*) "¡Hasta luego! Tengo clase." "Gracias" dice Josefina. (5) "<u>Gracias</u>. ¡Hasta luego!" dice José. "Hasta mañana" dice Josefina.

> **Answer Key:**
> (1) nueve y media (2) ¿Qué hora es? (3) Me llamo José. (4) ¿De dónde eres? (5) De nada.

8. Collaborate with students in establishing a list of guide words. **Note:** Guide words are a brief list of difficult words or phrases that occur in the story. Display the guide words.
9. Have students practice with partners using only the story's illustrations (page 3) and the guide words (if needed).
10. Have volunteers tell the story to the class. Students may use illustrations and guide words, if necessary.
11. Assessment: Have students record the story on audiocassettes. Students may use **only** the illustrations. Guide words may be used by students who need more direction. Evaluate the cassettes and include them in students' portfolios.
12. Collaborate with students in writing the story based on the illustrations. Write the story as students copy it.
13. Have partners invent a new story or alter the original story. Have them draw new or altered illustrations and then tell the story to the class.

Step 1	Gesturing New Vocabulary

Purpose: To introduce the new vocabulary.

1. Show the vocabulary list on the right, covering up the English and Gesture columns.

2. Introduce the first three words/ expressions.

3. Say the words one at a time and do the gestures.

4. Have students imitate the gestures silently.

5. Say the words and have students gesture with their eyes closed.

6. Test individual students randomly. Say a word and have students do the gesture. (If a word is not understood by several students, it must be included when teaching the following set of words.)

7. Do gestures and have students say the words.

8. Say the words and have students give the English equivalents.

9. Repeat this process (Steps 1-8) for the next set of three words until the vocabulary list is all presented.

10. Ask questions and have students answer.

   Sample Questions:
   ¿Cómo estás?
   ¿Tienes catarro?
   ¿Qué tienes en tus brazos?
   ¿Estás muy bien o muy mal por la mañana?
   ¿Llegas tarde a clase?

11. The following day review the vocabulary list using the above steps with increased speed.

12. You may also want to check students' comprehension by creating matching quizzes and fill-in-the-blank exercises.

Note: Some ways to invent gestures include referencing American Sign Language books, making them up or soliciting student input.

Spanish	English	Gesture
de la mañana	in the morning	Stretch and rub your eyes.
(ella) escucha	(she) listens to	Cup hands over your ears.
¿Cómo estás?	How are you? (informal)	Say *Estoy bien. ¿Cómo estás?*
Estoy muy mal.	I am not well.	Make a sad face.
¿Por qué?	Why?	Shrug your shoulders.
(ella) pregunta	(she) asks	Make a question mark in the air.
Me duele la cabeza.	My head hurts.	Hold your forehead as though in pain.
Lo siento.	I am sorry.	Tilt and shake your head.
¡Adiós!	Good bye!	Wave.
la boca	mouth	Point to your mouth.
Estoy regular.	I am okay.	Shake your hand back and forth.
Estás muy bien.	You are very well.	Make a big smile.
el catarro	cold	Cough and sneeze.
Me duele el estómago.	My stomach hurts.	Hold your stomach as though in pain.
perdón	excuse me	Gesture pushing somebody and say *Perdón.*
(él) corre	(he) runs	Mimic running.
los brazos	arms	Point to your arms.
¿Cómo está usted?	How are you? (formal)	Shrug your shoulders. Point to a teacher.
(ella) se tropieza	(she) trips	Mimic tripping.
(ella) va tarde	(She) is late	Put your hand on your head and look at your watch.

Additional Vocabulary

(ella) va, su amiga, armario, fuerte, (ella) grita, en voz baja, (ella) piensa, tan, (yo) tengo que, tomar, para llegar a, libros, de repente, se caen

Situations

1 Son las seis y media **de la mañana** y Pablo **está tarde** para el colegio. Pablo no quiere caminar al colegio. Pablo le dice a su mamá "**Estoy muy mal**. Tengo **catarro**". "**Lo siento**. Entonces, ¡toma el autobús!" le dice su mamá.

2 Pablo está en el colegio con su amigo Enrique. Pablo le **pregunta** a Enrique, "¿**Cómo estás**?" Enrique le responde "**Estoy regular**. **Me duele el estómago** y **la cabeza**". Pablo **escucha** bien y le dice "Lo siento..., bueno, tengo clase. ¡**Hasta pronto**!" "¡**Adiós**!" le dice Enrique.

3 Natalia **corre** a la clase de español. Ella lleva veinticinco hamburguesas grandes y una Coca Cola en **los brazos** para sus amigos, y una hamburguesa en **la boca**. Ella no **se tropieza**. Natalia entra y dice "¡Buenos días, Sra. Varela! ¿**Cómo está usted**?" "**Estoy muy bien**, gracias. ¡**Perdón**, Natalia!" le grita la profesora. La Sra. Varela le quita las hamburguesas. "¿**Por qué** me quita las hamburguesas?" le pregunta Natalia. La Sra. Varela le responde "¡No se puede comer hamburguesas en la clase de español, por favor!"

Advanced Story

La muchacha insensible

Son las ocho **de la mañana**. Alicia va con su amiga Marina a su armario mientras **escucha** música fuerte. Alicia le grita a su amiga "¿**Cómo estás**, Marina?" Marina le dice en voz baja "**Estoy muy mal**". "¿**Por qué**?" **pregunta** Alicia. "**Me duele la cabeza**" responde Marina. "**Lo siento**" grita Alicia. "¡**Adiós**!" Marina piensa "¡Qué muchacha tan insensible! Tengo que tomar una aspirina".

Alicia va a la cafetería. Tiene una hamburguesa grandísima en **la boca**. Le grita a un amigo con la hamburguesa en la boca "¡Hola, Francisco! ¿Cómo estás?" Francisco le dice "**Estoy regular**". "¿Por qué no **estás muy bien**?" pregunta Alicia. "Tengo **catarro** y **me duele el estómago**. ¡**Perdón**!" grita Francisco. Él **corre** al baño cuando ve la hamburguesa.

Alicia solamente tiene un minuto para llegar a la clase de español. Corre rápidamente a la clase con los libros en **los brazos**. De repente, Alicia ve a su profesora de español. "¡Buenos días, Sra. Rodríguez! ¿**Cómo está usted**?" "Estoy muy bien, gracias. ¡Hasta luego!" dice la profesora. Alicia **se tropieza** y sus libros se caen. Ella **va tarde** para la clase.

La muchacha insensible

Purpose: To use the vocabulary to tell a story.

1. Display the vocabulary list (page 5) in class. Students use the list as a reference.

2. Show illustrations (page 7), then tell the story. Have students follow along.

3. Pick student actors for the story.

4. Tell the story in an animated way. At the same time help student actors perform the story.

5. Ask **Yes/No Questions**.

> ¿Escucha Alicia música fuerte? (sí)
> ¿Está Marina muy bien? (no)
> ¿Tiene Alicia una pizza en la boca? (no)
> ¿Tiene Francisco catarro? (sí)
> ¿Le dice Alicia "¿Cómo estás?" a su profesora? (no)

6. Ask **Comprehension Questions** about the story.

> | | |
> |---|---|
> | ¿Qué hora es? | Son las ocho de la mañana. |
> | ¿Qué le pregunta Alicia a Marina? | ¿Cómo estás? |
> | ¿Qué problemas tiene Francisco? | Tiene catarro y le duele el estómago. |
> | ¿Qué tiene Alicia en los brazos? | Tiene unos libros. |
> | ¿Quién se tropieza? | Alicia se tropieza. |

7. Read the **Changed Story** and have students correct it.

> Son las ocho de la (1) <u>tarde</u>. Alicia va con su amiga Marina a su armario mientras escucha música fuerte. Alicia le grita a su amiga "¿Cómo estás, Marina?" Marina le dice en voz baja (2) "<u>Tengo catarro</u>". "¿Por qué?" pregunta Alicia. "Me duele la cabeza" responde Marina. "Lo siento" grita Alicia. "¡Adiós!" Marina piensa "¡Qué muchacha tan insensible! Tengo que tomar una aspirina".

> Alicia va a la cafetería. Tiene una hamburguesa grandísima en la boca. Le grita a un amigo con la hamburguesa en la boca "¡Hola, Francisco! (3) <u>¿De dónde eres?</u>" Francisco le dice "Estoy regular". "¿Por qué no estás muy bien?" pregunta Alicia. "Tengo catarro y (4) <u>estoy muy mal</u>. ¡Perdón!" grita Francisco. Él corre al baño cuando mira la hamburguesa.

> Alicia solamente tiene un minuto para llegar a la clase de español. Corre rápidamente a la clase con los libros en los brazos. De repente, Alicia ve a su profesora de español. "¡Buenos días, Sra. Rodríguez! ¿Cómo está usted?" "Estoy muy bien, gracias. ¡Hasta luego!" dice la profesora. Alicia se tropieza y sus libros se caen. Ella está (5) <u>mañana</u> para la clase.

> **Answer Key:**
> (1) mañana (2) Estoy muy mal. (3) ¿Cómo estás? (4) me duele el estómago (5) tarde

8. Collaborate with students in establishing a list of guide words. **Note:** Guide words are a brief list of difficult words or phrases that occur in the story. Display the guide words.

9. Have students practice with partners using only the story's illustrations (page 7) and the guide words (if needed).

10. Have volunteers tell the story to the class. Students may use illustrations and guide words, if necessary.

11. Assessment: Have students record the story on audiocassettes. Students may use **only** the illustrations. Guide words may be used by students who need more direction. Evaluate the cassettes and include them in students' portfolios.

12. Collaborate with students in writing the story based on the illustrations. Write the story as students copy it.

13. Have partners invent a new story or alter the original story. Have them draw new or altered illustrations and then tell the story to the class.

Basic Story

CAPÍTULO 2

Step 1 | Gesturing New Vocabulary

Purpose: To introduce the new vocabulary.

1. Show the vocabulary list on the right, covering up the English and Gesture columns.
2. Introduce the first three words/ expressions.
3. Say the words one at a time and do the gestures.
4. Have students imitate the gestures silently.
5. Say the words and have students gesture with their eyes closed.
6. Test individual students randomly. Say a word and have students do the gesture. (If a word is not understood by several students, it must be included when teaching the following set of words.)
7. Do gestures and have students say the words.
8. Say the words and have students give the English equivalents.
9. Repeat this process (Steps 1-8) for the next set of three words until the vocabulary list is all presented.
10. Ask questions and have students answer.

   Sample Questions:
   ¿Estás nervioso/a hoy?
   ¿Hablas por teléfono mucho?
   ¿Cuál es tu número de teléfono?
   ¿Necesitas estudiar mucho para tus clases?
   ¿Tienes una computadora?

11. The following day review the vocabulary list using the above steps with increased speed.
12. You may also want to check students' comprehension by creating matching quizzes and fill-in-the-blank exercises.

Note: Some ways to invent gestures include referencing American Sign Language books, making them up or soliciting student input.

Spanish	English	Gesture
(ella) está muy nerviosa	(she) is very nervous	Shake and look nervous.
piensa	(she) thinks	Point at your temple and look pensive.
estudiar	to study	Read a book intently.
(ella) necesita	(she) needs	Clench and shake your fists in desperation.
por teléfono	on the phone	Pretend to talk on the telephone.
No sé.	I do not know.	Shrug your shoulders.
el número	number	Dial a telephone number.
(ella) llama	(she) calls	Put your thumb and little finger by your ear and mouth.
hay	there is/there are	Say *No hay escuela hoy*.
la impresora láser	laser printer	Draw on the blackboard.
Te veo aquí (mañana).	I'll see you here (tomorrow).	Point to your eye and then to the floor.
(ella) va	(she) goes	Walk your fingers in the palm of your hand.
allí	there	Point to something.
nueva	new	Contrast something new with something old.
rápida	fast	Walk quickly.
terminar	to finish	Hold up your hands as though you just finished a race.
el correo electrónico	e-mail	Put an e-mail address on the blackboard.
mi amiga	my friend	Point to a girl and hold hands.
el poema de amor	love poem	Point to the poem on page 83 in the textbook and draw hearts.

© EMC   ***Navegando 1***   TPR Storytelling Manual   **Capítulo 2**   9

Situations

1 Pablo tiene un examen de biología. **Necesita estudiar** muchísimo para el examen. Entonces, **va** a (*name of coffee shop/library*) para estudiar. Estudia por diez minutos. De repente, ve a una muchacha muy, muy bonita de su clase de arte. Ahora **hay** un problema grande. No quiere estudiar más. Solamente quiere hablar con ella. Pero **está muy nervioso**.

2 Pablo va a su casa y escribe un **poema de amor** en su computadora **nueva.** Él **termina** en diez minutos. Su **impresora láser** es rápida, pero explota y entonces tiene que enviar el poema por **correo electrónico**.

3 Elena **piensa** que el poema de amor es muy romántico. Ella quiere hablar **por teléfono** con Pablo. Elena piensa "**¡No sé** su **número** de teléfono!" Ella **llama** a Información y pregunta su número de teléfono. Elena llama a Pablo y dice "¡Aló! Soy Elena. El poema es muy romántico, Pablo". Pablo le dice "Gracias. **Te veo aquí** mañana. Eres muy bonita". Elena le dice "Te veo **allí** mañana. ¡Vamos a ser amigos!" Pablo le dice "Sí, Elena. Vas a ser **mi amiga**".

Basic Story

Buenos amigos

Claudia **está muy nerviosa**. Ella **piensa** que Carlos es muy, muy inteligente, como Albert Einstein. Claudia quiere **estudiar** con Carlos. Ella **necesita** hablar con él **por teléfono**. Claudia dice "**No sé el número** de teléfono de Carlos". Claudia **llama** a Información. Información le dice "Su número de teléfono es el 6 40 30 86". Claudia llama a Carlos y le dice "¡Aló! ¿Carlos? Soy Claudia". Carlos le responde "¡Hola, Claudia! ¿Cómo estás? ¿**Hay** algún problema?" "Sí, tengo un problema. Necesito estudiar para mi clase de biología, pero mi computadora y mi **impresora láser** no funcionan. ¿Me permites usar tu computadora?" le pregunta Claudia. "Sí, con mucho gusto. **Te veo aquí**" le responde Carlos. Claudia **va** al apartamento de Carlos. "¡Hola, Carlos! ¿Dónde está tu computadora?" "**Allí** está mi computadora **nueva**. Es muy **rápida**. Pero necesito un minuto para **terminar** un **correo electrónico** para **mi amiga** de Ecuador. Le escribo un **poema de amor** a ella" dice Carlos. " ¡Eres muy romántico!" Claudia usa la computadora y la impresora láser. Al terminar Claudia dice "¡Muchas gracias, Carlos!" "¡De nada!" responde él. Carlos va con Claudia hasta su casa.

Purpose: To use the vocabulary to tell a story.

1. Display the vocabulary list (page 9) in class. Students use the list as a reference.

2. Show illustrations (page 11), then tell the story. Have students follow along.

3. Pick student actors for the story.

4. Tell the story in an animated way. At the same time help student actors perform the story.

5. Ask **Yes/No Questions**.

> ¿Necesita Claudia hablar con Carlos? (sí)
> ¿Llama Claudia a Información? (sí)
> ¿Estudia Claudia para la clase de arte? (no)
> ¿Es la computadora de Carlos rápida? (sí)
> ¿Escribe Carlos un poema de horror? (no)

6. Ask **Comprehension Questions** about the story.

¿Cómo está Claudia?	Claudia está muy nerviosa.
¿Cuál es el problema de Claudia?	Su computadora y su impresora láser no funcionan.
¿Por qué es la computadora de Carlos rápida?	Porque la computadora es nueva.
¿Qué necesita terminar Carlos?	Necesita terminar un correo electrónico.
¿Quién está en Ecuador?	Una amiga de Carlos.

7. Read the **Changed Story** and have students correct it.

> Claudia está muy (1) <u>rápida</u>. Ella piensa que Carlos es muy, muy inteligente, como Albert Einstein. Claudia quiere estudiar con Carlos. Ella necesita hablar con el (2) <u>por perdón</u>. Claudia dice "No sé el número de teléfono de Carlos". Claudia llama a Información. Información le dice "Su número de teléfono es el 6 40 30 86". Claudia llama a Carlos y le dice "¡Aló! ¿Carlos? Soy Claudia". Carlos le responde "¡Hola, Claudia! ¿Cómo estás? ¿Hay algún problema?" "Sí, tengo un problema. Necesito estudiar para mi clase de biología, pero mi computadora y mi (3) <u>teléfono</u> láser no funcionan. ¿Me permites usar tu computadora?" le pregunta Claudia. "Sí, con mucho gusto. Te veo aquí" le responde Carlos. Claudia va al apartamento de Carlos. "¡Hola, Carlos! ¿Dónde está tu computadora?" "Allí está mi computadora nueva. Es muy (4) <u>regular</u>. Pero necesito un minuto para terminar un correo electrónico para mi amiga de Ecuador. Le escribo un (5) <u>problema</u> de amor a ella" dice Carlos. " ¡Eres muy romántico!" Claudia usa la computadora y la impresora láser. Al terminar Claudia dice "¡Muchas gracias, Carlos!" "¡De nada!" responde él. Carlos va con Claudia hasta su casa.

> **Answer Key:**
> (1) nerviosa (2) por teléfono (3) impresora (4) rápida (5) poema

8. Collaborate with students in establishing a list of guide words. **Note:** Guide words are a brief list of difficult words or phrases that occur in the story. Display the guide words.

9. Have students practice with partners using only the story's illustrations (page 11) and the guide words (if needed).

10. Have volunteers tell the story to the class. Students may use illustrations and guide words, if necessary.

11. Assessment: Have students record the story on audiocassettes. Students may use **only** the illustrations. Guide words may be used by students who need more direction. Evaluate the cassettes and include them in students' portfolios.

12. Collaborate with students in writing the story based on the illustrations. Write the story as students copy it.

13. Have partners invent a new story or alter the original story. Have them draw new or altered illustrations and then tell the story to the class.

Step 1 — Gesturing New Vocabulary

Purpose: To introduce the new vocabulary.

1. Show the vocabulary list on the right, covering up the English and Gesture columns.

2. Introduce the first three words/expressions.

3. Say the words one at a time and do the gestures.

4. Have students imitate the gestures silently.

5. Say the words and have students gesture with their eyes closed.

6. Test individual students randomly. Say a word and have students do the gesture. (If a word is not understood by several students, it must be included when teaching the following set of words.)

7. Do gestures and have students say the words.

8. Say the words and have students give the English equivalents.

9. Repeat this process (Steps 1-8) for the next set of three words until the vocabulary list is all presented.

10. Ask questions and have students answer.

   Sample Questions:
   ¿Qué tienes en tu mochila?
   ¿Qué necesitas para la escuela?
   ¿Tienes papel hoy?
   ¿Cuántos/as chicos/as hay en la clase de español?
   ¿Cuál es tu revista favorita?

11. The following day review the vocabulary list using the above steps with increased speed.

12. You may also want to check students' comprehension by creating matching quizzes and fill-in-the-blank exercises.

Note: Some ways to invent gestures include referencing American Sign Language books, making them up or soliciting student input.

Spanish	English	Gesture
la mochila	backpack	Point to a backpack.
roja	red	Point to something red.
amarilla	yellow	Point to something yellow.
caramba	wow	Look surprised.
pesada	heavy	Pick up a heavy item.
la revista	magazine	Show a magazine.
el papel	paper	Point to a piece of paper.
los lápices	pencils	Hold up pencils.
los bolígrafos	pens	Hold up pens.
las reglas	rulers	Hold up rulers.
los borradores	erasers	Hold up erasers.
las chicas	girls	Point to some girls.
los chicos	boys	Point to some boys.
los libros	books	Point to books.
la puerta	door	Point to a door.

Additional Vocabulary

fuera, colegio, me gusta, grande, bonita, pequeña, (ella) toma, solamente, (yo) llevo, diario, maquillaje, (tú) llevas, (ella) abre, confundida, (ella) le pregunta, tantas cosas, me compran, las olvidan, entonces, (yo) gano, todos los días, trabajar, empresaria, (tú) cargas, (yo) cargo, novio, (él) carga, (ellas) oyen, ruido, cobra, (ella) corre

Situations

1 Josefina y Alicia están en Kinder. Josefina le dice a Alicia "Mira, tú tienes una **mochila roja** y yo tengo una mochila **amarilla**. ¡Quiero tu mochila roja!" (*Girls fighting over their backpacks.*) Josefina toma la mochila roja de Alicia y dice "¡Ay, **caramba**! Tu mochila está muy **pesada**. No la quiero. Quiero mi mochila amarilla. ¡Adiós!"

2 Hay una profesora en el colegio que tiene todas las cosas que necesita en su clase. Tiene muchos **lápices**, **bolígrafos** y **reglas** para sus estudiantes. En este momento ella escribe y escribe en la pizarra hasta que no hay más espacio en ella. La profesora necesita **el borrador**, pero no lo ve en la clase. "¡Ay, caramba! ¿Dónde está mi borrador?" Ella va a su oficina, a la cafetería y a los armarios de los estudiantes, pero el borrador tampoco está allí. Finalmente lo ve en su taza de café.

3 Pablo tiene hoy su primer día de clases en el colegio. En este momento él está con su mamá en **la puerta** de su casa. Pablo le dice a su mamá "Estoy muy nervioso. El colegio es muy grande y hay muchos **chicos** y **chicas** allí". "Vas a estar bien, mijito. ¿Tienes todo lo que necesitas?" "Sí, mamá. Tengo mis **libros** de historia, matemáticas y arte." "Aquí tienes **papel** y tu **revista** favorita." Pablo está contento. "¡Hasta luego, mamá!" "¡Adiós!"

Advanced Story

La cobra en la mochila

Gabriela y Gloria están fuera del colegio. Gabriela le dice a Gloria "Me gusta tu **mochila roja.** Es muy grande y muy bonita. Yo tengo una mochila **amarilla,** pero es pequeña". Gabriela toma la mochila de Gloria y grita "¡Ay, **caramba**! Tu mochila está muy **pesada**. En mi mochila solamente llevo una **revista**, mi diario, **papel** y maquillaje. ¿Qué llevas tú?" Gloria abre su mochila y dice "Pues, llevo cien **lápices**, **bolígrafos**, **reglas** y **borradores**". Gabriela confundida le pregunta "¿Por qué llevas tantas cosas en tu mochila?" "Porque las **chicas** y los **chicos** me compran estas cosas a mí cuando las olvidan. Entonces, gano millones de pesos todos los días y no necesito trabajar en (*name of workplace*)." "¡Eres una empresaria, Gloria!" dice Gabriela. "¿Tienes más en tu mochila?" "Sí, tengo mis **libros** de historia, matemáticas y arte" responde Gloria. "¿Cómo cargas tú con esa mochila?" pregunta Gabriela. "No cargo mi mochila. Mi novio, Roberto, la carga." De repente, las chicas oyen un ruido en la mochila. "¿Qué es ese ruido?" pregunta Gabriela. "Oh....es solamente mi cobra, Susanita. Ella es muy, muy...." "¡Ah!" grita Gabriela y corre por **la puerta**.

La cobra en la mochila

Purpose: To use the vocabulary to tell a story.

1. Display the vocabulary list (page 13) in class. Students use the list as a reference.

2. Show illustrations (page 15), then tell the story. Have students follow along.

3. Pick student actors for the story.

4. Tell the story in an animated way. At the same time help student actors perform the story.

5. Ask **Yes/No Questions**.

> ¿Está pesada la mochila de Gabriela? (no)
> ¿Lleva Gabriela una revista, un diario, papel y maquillaje en su mochila? (sí)
> ¿Le compran los profesores cosas a Gloria? (no)
> ¿Lleva Gloria libros en su mochila? (sí)
> ¿Lleva Gloria un elefante en su mochila? (no)

6. Ask **Comprehension Questions** about the story.

¿Qué lleva Gloria en su mochila?	Lleva lápices, bolígrafos, reglas, borradores, libros y una cobra.
¿Quién le compra las cosas a Gloria?	Las chicas y los chicos le compran las cosas a Gloria.
¿Cuánto dinero gana Gloria?	Gloria gana millones de pesos.
¿Quién carga la mochila de Gloria?	El novio de Gloria carga la mochila.
¿Qué tipo de animal lleva Gloria en la mochila?	Lleva una cobra en la mochila.

7. Read the **Changed Story** and have students correct it.

> Gabriela y Gloria están fuera del colegio. Gabriela le dice a Gloria "Me gusta tu (1) <u>revista</u> roja. Es muy grande y muy bonita. Yo tengo una mochila amarilla, pero es pequeña". Gabriela toma la mochila de Gloria y grita "¡Ay, caramba! Tu mochila está muy (2) <u>nueva</u>. En mi mochila solamente llevo una revista, mi diario, papel y maquillaje. ¿Qué llevas tú?" Gloria abre su mochila y dice "Pues, llevo (3) <u>puertas</u>, bolígrafos, reglas y borradores". Gabriela confundida le pregunta "¿Por qué llevas tantas cosas en tu mochila?" "Porque las chicas y los chicos me compran estas cosas a mí cuando las olvidan. Entonces, gano millones de pesos todos los días y no necesito trabajar en (*name of workplace*)." "¡Eres una empresaria, Gloria!" dice Gabriela. "¿Tienes más en tu mochila?" "Sí, tengo mis (4) <u>reglas</u> de historia, matemáticas y arte" responde Gloria. "¿Cómo cargas tú con esa mochila?" pregunta Gabriela. "No cargo mi mochila. Mi novio, Roberto, la carga." De repente, las chicas oyen un ruido en la mochila. "¿Qué es ese ruido?" pregunta Gabriela. "Oh....es solamente mi cobra, Susanita. Ella es muy, muy...." "¡Ah!" grita Gabriela y corre por la (5) <u>mochila</u>.

> **Answer Key:**
> (1) mochila (2) pesada (3) lápices (4) libros (5) puerta

8. Collaborate with students in establishing a list of guide words. **Note:** Guide words are a brief list of difficult words or phrases that occur in the story. Display the guide words.

9. Have students practice with partners using only the story's illustrations (page 15) and the guide words (if needed).

10. Have volunteers tell the story to the class. Students may use illustrations and guide words, if necessary.

11. Assessment: Have students record the story on audiocassettes. Students may use **only** the illustrations. Guide words may be used by students who need more direction. Evaluate the cassettes and include them in students' portfolios.

12. Collaborate with students in writing the story based on the illustrations. Write the story as students copy it.

13. Have partners invent a new story or alter the original story. Have them draw new or altered illustrations and then tell the story to the class.

	Spanish	English	Gesture

Step 1 — Gesturing New Vocabulary

Purpose: To introduce the new vocabulary.

1. Show the vocabulary list on the right, covering up the English and Gesture columns.

2. Introduce the first three words/ expressions.

3. Say the words one at a time and do the gestures.

4. Have students imitate the gestures silently.

5. Say the words and have students gesture with their eyes closed.

6. Test individual students randomly. Say a word and have students do the gesture. (If a word is not understood by several students, it must be included when teaching the following set of words.)

7. Do gestures and have students say the words.

8. Say the words and have students give the English equivalents.

9. Repeat this process (Steps 1-8) for the next set of three words until the vocabulary list is all presented.

10. Ask questions and have students answer.

   Sample Questions:
   ¿Tomas un autobús para ir al colegio?
   ¿Cuándo vas al médico?
   ¿Dónde está tu casa?
   ¿Tomas agua mineral o agua de la llave?
   ¿Te gusta el pescado y la ensalada?

11. The following day review the vocabulary list using the above steps with increased speed.

12. You may also want to check students' comprehension by creating matching quizzes and fill-in-the-blank exercises.

Note: Some ways to invent gestures include referencing American Sign Language books, making them up or soliciting student input.

Spanish	English	Gesture
en avión	by plane	Spread your arms and pretend to fly like a plane.
(ellas) llegan	(they) arrive	Walk up to some one and say *llegar.*
(ellas) toman un autobús	(they) take a bus	Pretend you are taking a bus.
a pie	on foot	Walk while pointing to your feet.
cerca de	close to	Say (place) *está cerca de la escuela.*
(ellas) comen	(they) eat	Motion eating.
la ensalada	salad	Point to the picture on page 117 in the textbook.
el pescado	fish	Point to the picture on page 117 in the textbook.
solamente	only	Place index finger in the air and move your hand in a circle one time.
(ellas) toman agua	(they) drink water	Gesture as if you are drinking water.
le duele	it hurts	Point to your stomach and groan.
el estómago	stomach	Point to your stomach.
el baño	bathroom	Point to the bathroom.
la policía	police	Make a police car sound.
lejos de	far from	Say (place) *está lejos de la escuela.*
la biblioteca	library	Point to the library.
(ella) grita	(she) shouts	Mimic shouting.
¡Claro!	Of course!	Say *Claro*—Of course.
la médica	the (female) doctor	Point to the doctor on page 90 in the textbook.
el agua de la llave	tap water	Pretend you are turning on a faucet and filling a glass with water.

Situations

1 Juan y una amiga **toman un autobús** para ir al colegio. De repente, tienen una colisión con otro autobús. **La policía** va al accidente. A Juan **le duele el estómago** y necesita ir al hospital. **La médica** le dice "**Tome agua** y esta medicina".

2 Carlos y Gabriela van a un restaurante. El restaurante es muy romántico. Gabriela va al **baño** por un momento. Una chica le dice a Carlos "Aquí está el menú. ¿Qué **comen** hoy?" Carlos le responde "**Pescado** y **ensalada**, por favor". "¿Y para tomar?" "**Solamente agua de la llave**, por favor" dice Carlos. Gabriela retorna del baño. El pescado y la ensalada **llegan** y ella **grita** "¡Ah! ¡Yo no como pescado! Soy vegetariana". Ella le pasa el pescado a Carlos y come solamente la ensalada y toma un vaso de agua mineral.

3 Miguel va **en avión** a Colombia de vacaciones. Cuando llega a Colombia, Miguel va al hotel **a pie**. Pero tiene un problema: no encuentra el hotel. Va a **la biblioteca** y pregunta "¿Dónde está el Hotel San Mateo? ¿Está muy **lejos de** aquí?" "No, no. El hotel está **cerca de** aquí." Miguel mira al mapa y le responde "¡**Claro**! Está aquí". *(Miguel points to the map.)*

Basic Story

Vacaciones con problemas

Jenny y su mamá van **en avión** de Miami a Ciudad de México. Cuando **llegan** a Ciudad de México **toman un autobús** para ir al hotel. Van **a pie** a un restaurante que hay **cerca del** hotel. **Comen ensalada**, **pescado** y **solamente toman agua**. Después de comer, a Jenny **le duele** mucho **el estómago**. Ella va al **baño.** Su mamá está muy, muy nerviosa y llama a **la policía**. Un policía responde "¡Aló! ¿Cuál es el problema?" La mamá le dice "Habla la señora Smith. Necesito un médico. ¿Dónde está el hospital? Estoy en el hotel San Gabriel". El policía le dice "El hospital no está muy **lejos del** hotel. Está cerca de **la biblioteca**". La mamá le dice "Muchas gracias, señor" y luego llama a un taxi. El taxi llega al hotel. Jenny y su mamá entran al taxi. La mamá **grita** "¡Al hospital, por favor, señor!" El señor le dice "¡**Claro**! Vamos a estar en el hospital en cinco minutos". Jenny vomita en el taxi. El señor dice "¡Ay caramba!" Jenny dice "Lo siento mucho, señor". Ya en el hospital **la médica** le pregunta a Jenny "¿Tomaste **agua de la llave**?" Jenny le responde "Sí, doctora". "En el futuro solamente debes tomar agua mineral" dice la médica.

Purpose: To use the vocabulary to tell a story.

1. Display the vocabulary list (page 17) in class. Students use the list as a reference.

2. Show illustrations (page 19), then tell the story. Have students follow along.

3. Pick student actors for the story.

4. Tell the story in an animated way. At the same time help student actors perform the story.

5. Ask **Yes/No Questions**.

   ¿Van Jenny y su mamá en autobús a Miami? (no)
   ¿Come Jenny una hamburguesa? (no)
   ¿Está el hospital muy cerca del hotel? (sí)
   ¿Van Jenny y su mamá a caballo al hospital? (no)
   ¿Le dice la médica a Jenny que solamente tome agua de la llave? (no)

6. Ask **Comprehension Questions** about the story.

¿Cómo van Jenny y su mamá a México?	Van en avión.
¿Qué hay cerca del hotel?	Hay un restaurante cerca del hotel.
¿Qué hace la mamá cuando está nerviosa?	Llama a la policía.
¿Dónde está el hospital?	Está cerca de la biblioteca.
¿Qué le dice la médica a Jenny?	Le dice "Solamente toma agua mineral".

7. Read the **Changed Story** and have students correct it.

   Jenny y su mamá van en avión de Miami a Ciudad de México. Cuando llegan a Ciudad de México toman un autobús para ir al hotel. Van (1) en tren a un restaurante que hay cerca del hotel. Comen (2) burrito de frijoles y solamente toman (3) jugo de naranja. Después de comer, a Jenny le duele mucho el estómago. Su mamá está muy, muy nerviosa y llama a la policía. Un policía responde "¡Aló! ¿Cuál es el problema?" La mamá le dice "Habla la señora Smith. Necesito un médico. ¿Dónde está el hospital? Estoy en el hotel San Gabriel". El policía le dice "El hospital no está muy lejos del hotel. Está cerca de la (4) cafetería". La mamá le dice "Muchas gracias, señor" y luego llama a un taxi. El taxi llega al hotel. Jenny y su mamá entran al taxi. La mamá grita"¡Al hospital, por favor, señor!" El señor le dice "¡Claro! Vamos a estar en el hospital en cinco minutos". Jenny vomita en el taxi. El señor dice "¡Ay caramba!" Jenny dice "Lo siento mucho, señor". Ya en el hospital la (5) dentista le pregunta a Jenny "¿Tomaste agua de la llave?" Jenny le responde "Sí, doctora". "En el futuro solamente debes tomar agua mineral" dice la médica.

   Answer Key:
   (1) a pie (2) ensalada, pescado (3) agua (4) biblioteca (5) médica

8. Collaborate with students in establishing a list of guide words. **Note:** Guide words are a brief list of difficult words or phrases that occur in the story. Display the guide words.

9. Have students practice with partners using only the story's illustrations (page 19) and the guide words (if needed).

10. Have volunteers tell the story to the class. Students may use illustrations and guide words, if necessary.

11. Assessment: Have students record the story on audiocassettes. Students may use **only** the illustrations. Guide words may be used by students who need more direction. Evaluate the cassettes and include them in students' portfolios.

12. Collaborate with students in writing the story based on the illustrations. Write the story as students copy it.

13. Have partners invent a new story or alter the original story. Have them draw new or altered illustrations and then tell the story to the class.

Step 1 | Gesturing New Vocabulary

Purpose: To introduce the new vocabulary.

1. Show the vocabulary list on the right, covering up the English and Gesture columns.

2. Introduce the first three words/ expressions.

3. Say the words one at a time and do the gestures.

4. Have students imitate the gestures silently.

5. Say the words and have students gesture with their eyes closed.

6. Test individual students randomly. Say a word and have students do the gesture. (If a word is not understood by several students, it must be included when teaching the following set of words.)

7. Do gestures and have students say the words.

8. Say the words and have students give the English equivalents.

9. Repeat this process (Steps 1-8) for the next set of three words until the vocabulary list is all presented.

10. Ask questions and have students answer.

   Sample Questions:
   ¿Tomas jugo de naranja?
   ¿Siempre vas en metro?
   ¿Siempre eres simpático/a?
   ¿Comes tacos de pollo?
   ¿Quieres comer frijoles negros?

11. The following day review the vocabulary list using the above steps with increased speed.

12. You may also want to check students' comprehension by creating matching quizzes and fill-in-the-blank exercises.

Note: Some ways to invent gestures include referencing American Sign Language books, making them up or soliciting student input.

Spanish	English	Gesture
la taquería	taco restaurant	Hold a taco and say the name of a Mexican restaurant.
el jugo de naranja	orange juice	Draw an orange on the blackboard and hold up a cup.
Tanto gusto.	So glad to meet you.	Shake hands and smile.
Encantado.	I'm delighted.	Shake hands and smile.
simpática	nice	Point to a girl and say *Ella es simpática.*
pues	well	Say *pues*—well.
el mesero	waiter	Hold a tray and serve someone.
el arroz con pollo	chicken with rice	Show a picture of chicken with rice.
los frijoles negros	black beans	Show a picture of black beans.
siempre	always	Say *siempre*—always.
pero	but	Say *pero*—but.
la comida	food	Motion toward your lips and move your mouth.
caminar	to walk	Walk around as you point toward your feet and say *caminar.*
bueno	okay, well	Say *bueno*—okay.
(él) besa	(he) kisses	Kiss the back of your hand.
la mano	hand	Point to your hand and say *mano.*
es que	well, it's just that	Say *es que*—well.
en metro	by subway	Point to the illustration of the *metro* on page 100 in the textbook.

Additional Vocabulary

sola, se acerca, me permites, sentarme, (él) se sienta, (ella) se pone, poco, toca, canta, (él) susurra, querer, (ella) no puede oírle, (ellos) pagan, (ellos) salen, hace buen tiempo, ambiente, (ella) se va

Situations

1 Julia y su amiga, María, van **en metro** a la escuela. De repente, Julia ve a su novio, Pablo. "¡Hola, Pablo!" grita Julia. Pablo se acerca a ella y le dice "¡Buenos días! ¿Por qué estás aquí?" Ella responde "**Es que siempre** voy en metro a la escuela". Pablo le pregunta a María "¿Cómo te llamas?" "Me llamo María." "**Tanto gusto**" le dice Pablo. "**Encantado**" le responde María. Él le **besa la mano** a María. Julia le grita a Pablo "¡No eres **simpático** y ya no eres mi novio!"

2 La señora Maldonado y el señor García van en avión a Buenos Aires. Ellos van en un avión de los Estados Unidos y no quieren hamburguesas de **comida**. La señora Maldonado le dice a un señor de la aerolínea "¿Dónde está el menú? Quiero **arroz con pollo**". "Y yo quiero **frijoles negros**" dice el señor García. "Lo siento, **pero** no tenemos comida mexicana en el avión" responde el señor. "¡Ay, caramba!" dicen el señor García y la señora Maldonado.

3 La familia Martínez va a una **taquería** para comer. Ellos llaman al **mesero,** pero él nunca oye. "¡Ay, papá, quiero comer!" dice Pablito. La mamá dice "Vamos a otra taquería". "No quiero **caminar** más" dice Pablito. El papá dice "**Pues**, yo sé de otro restaurante cerca de aquí y tiene unos tacos de pollo deliciosos y un **jugo de naranja** excelente. La mamá dice "**Bueno**, vamos a ese restaurante".

Advanced Story

Pobre Jaime

Vicky es de Chicago y está sola en una **taquería**. Ella toma un **jugo de naranja**. Un muchacho se acerca a ella y le dice "¡Buenas noches, señorita! Me llamo Jaime". "**Tanto gusto**. Me llamo Vicky." "**Encantado**. Eres una muchacha muy **simpática**. ¿Me permites sentarme aquí?" "**Pues**...sí. Está bien." Él se sienta muy cerca de ella. Ella se pone un poco nerviosa. **El mesero** se acerca a ellos y les dice "Aquí está el menú". "No, gracias. Yo sé qué vamos a comer. Queremos **arroz con pollo, frijoles negros** y tacos de pollo, por favor" dice Jaime. El mariachi toca y canta música romántica. Jaime le susurra "Te voy a querer **siempre**, Vicky". **Pero** Vicky no puede oírle, porque la música está muy fuerte. **La comida** llega y ellos comen. "¿Quieres **caminar** por el parque?" le pregunta Jaime a Vicky. "**Bueno**, sí." Ellos pagan y salen de la taquería. Hace buen tiempo y el ambiente es muy romántico. Jaime le **besa la mano** a Vicky. Vicky le dice "¡No! ¡No! Eres un chico muy simpático, pero **es que** ya tengo un novio en Chicago. Lo siento mucho. ¡Adiós, Jaime!" Ella se va para el hotel **en metro**.

Pobre Jaime

Purpose: To use the vocabulary to tell a story.

1. Display the vocabulary list (page 21) in class. Students use the list as a reference.

2. Show illustrations (page 23), then tell the story. Have students follow along.

3. Pick student actors for the story.

4. Tell the story in an animated way. At the same time help student actors perform the story.

5. Ask **Yes/No Questions**.

   ¿Toma Vicky jugo de naranja? (sí)
   ¿Comen Jaime y Vicky tacos y burritos? (no)
   ¿Es Jaime simpático? (sí)
   ¿Tiene Vicky un novio en Los Ángeles? (no)
   ¿Se va Vicky en taxi? (no)

6. Ask **Comprehension Questions** about the story.

¿Dónde come Vicky?	Come en una taquería.
¿Qué comen Vicky y Jaime?	Comen arroz con pollo, frijoles negros y tacos de pollo.
¿Por qué no puede Vicky oírle?	Porque la música está muy fuerte.
¿Quién está en Chicago?	El novio de Vicky está en Chicago.
¿En qué se va Vicky para el hotel?	Se va en metro.

7. Read the **Changed Story** and have students correct it.

   Vicky es de Chicago y está sola en una taquería. Ella toma (1) <u>agua mineral</u>. Un muchacho se acerca a ella y le dice "¡Buenas noches, señorita! Me llamo Jaime". "Tanto gusto. Me llamo Vicky." (2) "<u>Adiós.</u>" "Eres una muchacha muy simpática. ¿Me permites sentarme aquí?" "Pues...sí. Está bien." Él se sienta muy cerca de ella. Ella se pone un poco nerviosa. El (3) <u>dentista</u> se acerca a ellos y les dice "Aquí está el menú". "No, gracias. Yo sé que vamos a comer. Queremos arroz con pollo, frijoles negros y tacos de pollo, por favor" dice Jaime. El mariachi toca y canta música romántica. Jaime le susurra "Te voy a querer (4) <u>nunca</u>, Vicky". Pero Vicky no puede oírle, porque la música está muy fuerte. La comida llega y ellos comen. "¿Quieres caminar por el parque?" le pregunta Jaime a Vicky. "Bueno, sí." Ellos pagan y salen de la taquería. Hace buen tiempo y el ambiente es muy romántico. Jaime le besa la mano a Vicky. Vicky le dice "¡No! ¡No! Eres un chico muy simpático, pero es que ya tengo un novio en Chicago. Lo siento mucho. ¡Adiós, Jaime!" Ella se va para el hotel (5) <u>en mesero</u>.

   Answer Key:
   (1) un jugo de naranja (2) Encantado. (3) mesero (4) siempre (5) en metro

8. Collaborate with students in establishing a list of guide words. **Note:** Guide words are a brief list of difficult words or phrases that occur in the story. Display the guide words.

9. Have students practice with partners using only the story's illustrations (page 23) and the guide words (if needed).

10. Have volunteers tell the story to the class. Students may use illustrations and guide words, if necessary.

11. Assessment: Have students record the story on audiocassettes. Students may use **only** the illustrations. Guide words may be used by students who need more direction. Evaluate the cassettes and include them in students' portfolios.

12. Collaborate with students in writing the story based on the illustrations. Write the story as students copy it.

13. Have partners invent a new story or alter the original story. Have them draw new or altered illustrations and then tell the story to the class.

Step 1 | Gesturing New Vocabulary

Purpose: To introduce the new vocabulary.

1. Show the vocabulary list on the right, covering up the English and Gesture columns.

2. Introduce the first three words/ expressions.

3. Say the words one at a time and do the gestures.

4. Have students imitate the gestures silently.

5. Say the words and have students gesture with their eyes closed.

6. Test individual students randomly. Say a word and have students do the gesture. (If a word is not understood by several students, it must be included when teaching the following set of words.)

7. Do gestures and have students say the words.

8. Say the words and have students give the English equivalents.

9. Repeat this process (Steps 1-8) for the next set of three words until the vocabulary list is all presented.

10. Ask questions and have students answer.

> **Sample Questions:**
> *¿Cómo se llama tu padre/madre?*
> *¿A qué hora haces tu tarea?*
> *¿Eres atlético/a?*
> *¿Juegas al tenis o al béisbol?*
> *¿Qué clase es difícil para ti?*

11. The following day review the vocabulary list using the above steps with increased speed.

12. You may also want to check students' comprehension by creating matching quizzes and fill-in-the-blank exercises.

Note: Some ways to invent gestures include referencing American Sign Language books, making them up or soliciting student input.

Spanish	English	Gesture
(ellos) piden	(they) ask	Have a group of students shrug shoulders.
(ellos) van de compras	(they) go shopping	Say name of a shopping center an walk.
el padre	father	Point to the father on page 134 in the textbook.
nada	nothing	Make a sweeping gesture with your hand.
la madre	mother	Point to the mother on page 134 in the textbook.
amable	nice	Point to a nice student.
(ellas) juegan	(they) play	Bounce a ball.
el tenis	tennis	Swing a racket.
el béisbol	baseball	Catch a baseball.
atlético	athletic	Say the name of famous athletic person.
divertido	fun	Name a fun event or activity.
(yo) tengo que	(I) have to	Hit the palm of your left hand with the fist of your right hand emphatically.
la tarea	homework	Point to a homework assignment written on the board.
(ella) oye	(she) listens	Point to your ear.
la radio	radio	Point to a radio.
difícil	difficult	Say the name of a hard class.
después de	after	Draw a school day time line and demonstrate "after school."
cómico	funny	Say the name of a famous comedian.
(él) le da	(he) gives her	Give something to a student.
generoso	generous	Demonstrate giving a lot of money.

Situations

1 En quince días es el aniversario de **la madre** y **el padre** de Ana. Su padre quiere comprar un presente. La madre de Ana le **pide** un caballo de presente. El padre dice "Muy bien". El padre **va de compras** a un rancho en Kentucky para comprar el caballo. Él compra un excelente caballo de un millón de dolares. El padre **le da** el caballo a la madre y ella grita "¡Ay, caramba! ¡Qué bien! ¡Eres muy **generoso**!" Ahora hay un problema. La familia de Ana no tiene un establo para el caballo y él tiene que vivir en el jardín. El caballo come las plantas y destruye todo en el jardín. Ana, furiosa, le pregunta a su mamá "¿Ahora **tengo que** limpiar siempre el jardín?" La mamá le responde "¡No! ¡No! El caballo va ahora mismo para Kentucky".

2 Treinta chicos y chicas muy **atléticos** de *(name of school)* van a Venus para jugar en unos juegos olímpicos. Los chicos y las chicas de Venus tienen que jugar con los chicos y las chicas de *(name of school)* por quince días. Ellos **juegan** al **tenis** y al **béisbol**. Los chicos de Venus tienen cuatro manos muy grandes y fuertes y no necesitan usar **nada** para jugar al tenis o al béisbol, ni raquetas ni bates. Los chicos de *(name of school)* están muy nerviosos, pero los chicos de Venus son muy **divertidos** y **amables** y **después de** jugar por dos horas, todos están muy contentos.

3 Jorge está en su casa con su amiga, Andrea. Ellos hacen la tarea de matemáticas. Jorge está muy nervioso porque tiene problemas con la tarea. Él le dice a su amiga "**La tarea** de matemáticas es muy, muy **difícil**, ¿no?" Andrea le responde "Eres muy **cómico.** Yo no tengo problemas con la tarea de matemáticas". Ellos hablan de la tarea por tres horas. Cuando Jorge y Andrea hablan, ellos **oyen** en **la radio** que la banda favorita de Andrea va a estar en *(name of city)* mañana. Andrea dice "¡Quiero ir al concierto de mi banda favorita, pero no tengo dinero!" Ellos terminan la tarea y Jorge está muy contento. Jorge le dice "Muchas gracias, Andrea". Jorge le da una rosa y le dice "Mañana vamos al concierto de tu banda favorita". Andrea está muy contenta y grita "¡Que bueno! Eres muy dulce, Jorge".

Basic Story

Tres amigos

El viernes hay una fiesta en el colegio de Teresa. Tres amigos de Teresa, Diego, Fernando y Ricardo, le **piden** ir a la fiesta con ella, pero ella no sabe con quién ir. Teresa y su mamá **van de compras** al centro el sábado. Allí Teresa ve a Diego con su **padre** y le dice "¡Hola, Diego! ¿Qué compras?" "¡Hola, Teresa! **Nada**. No compro nada. ¡Adiós, Teresa!" responde Diego. **La madre** le dice "Él es muy **amable**, Teresa." "Sí, mamá" responde ella.

El miércoles Teresa y su amiga, Mercedes, **juegan** al **tenis** en el parque. Allí ellas ven a Fernando. Él juega al **béisbol** con sus amigos. Mercedes le dice a Teresa "Él es muy **atlético** y **divertido**, ¿verdad?" Teresa le responde "¡Sí, sí es muy atlético y divertido, Mercedes! Bueno, son las siete y **tengo que** hacer **la tarea**. ¡Hasta mañana, Mercedes!" "¡Adiós, Teresa!"

Teresa hace la tarea de matemáticas y **oye la radio**. Ricardo llama a Teresa. "¡Aló, Teresa! Tengo problemas con la tarea de matemáticas. Es muy **difícil**...." **Después de** hablar por dos horas Teresa le dice "Eres muy **cómico**, Ricardo".

El jueves en el colegio Diego **le da** un regalo a Teresa. Ella le dice "Muchas gracias. Eres muy **generoso**. ¿Sabes? Voy a la fiesta contigo". Diego está muy feliz.

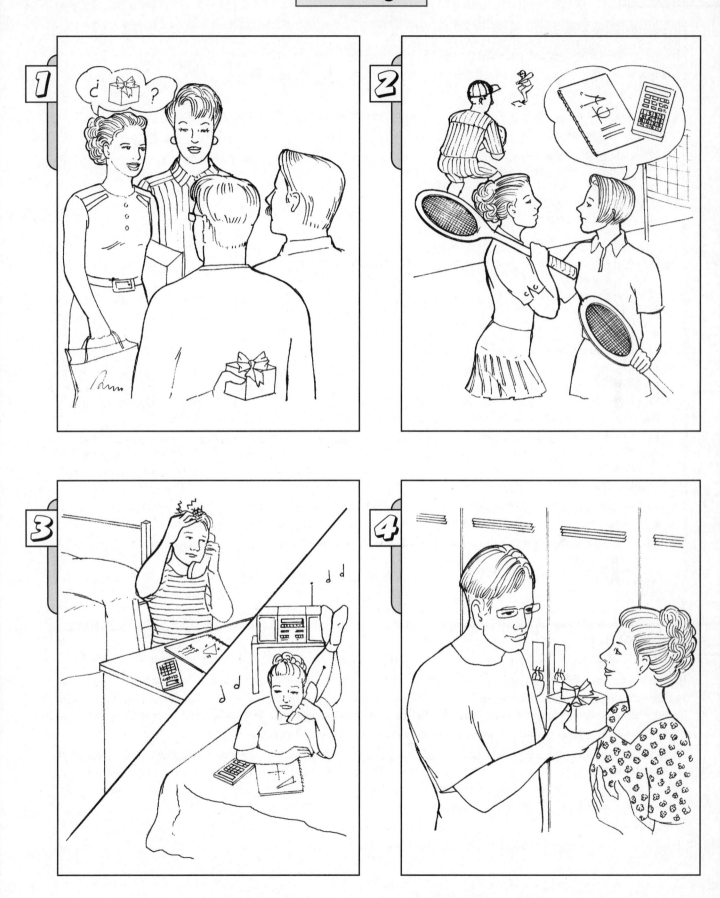

Tres amigos

Purpose: To use the vocabulary to tell a story.

1. Display the vocabulary list (page 25) in class. Students use the list as a reference.

2. Show illustrations (page 27), then tell the story. Have students follow along.

3. Pick student actors for the story.

4. Tell the story in an animated way. At the same time help student actors perform the story.

5. Ask **Yes/No Questions**.

> ¿Hay una fiesta el miércoles? (no)
> ¿Van de compras Teresa y su padre? (no)
> ¿Juega Fernando al tenis? (no)
> ¿Oye Teresa la radio? (sí)
> ¿Le da Diego un presente a Teresa? (sí)

6. Ask **Comprehension Questions** about the story.

> ¿Qué hacen Teresa y su mamá el sábado?　　Ellas van de compras.
> ¿Qué dice su madre de Diego?　　Dice que él es muy amable.
> ¿Qué hacen Teresa y su amiga en el parque?　　Ellas juegan al tenis.
> ¿Qué tiene que hacer Teresa a las siete?　　Ella tiene que hacer la tarea.
> ¿Qué oye Teresa cuando hace la tarea?　　Ella oye la radio.

7. Read the **Changed Story** and have students correct it.

> El viernes hay (1) <u>un examen</u> en el colegio de Teresa. Tres amigos de Teresa, Diego, Fernando y Ricardo, le piden ir a la fiesta con ella, pero ella no sabe con quién ir. Teresa y su mamá van de compras al centro el sábado. Allí Teresa ve a Diego con su padre y le dice "¡Hola, Diego! ¿Qué compras?" "¡Hola, Teresa! Nada. No compro nada. ¡Adiós, Teresa!" responde Diego. La madre le dice "Él es muy (2) <u>romántico</u>, Teresa." "Sí, mamá" responde ella.

> El miércoles Teresa y su amiga, Mercedes, juegan al (3) <u>básquetbol</u> en el parque. Allí ellas ven a Fernando. Él juega al béisbol con sus amigos. Mercedes le dice a Teresa "Él es muy (4) <u>guapo</u> y divertido, ¿verdad?" Teresa le responde "¡Sí, sí es muy atlético y divertido, Mercedes! Bueno, son las siete y tengo que hacer la tarea. ¡Hasta mañana, Mercedes!" "¡Adiós, Teresa!"

> Teresa hace la tarea de matemáticas y (5) <u>baila</u>. Ricardo llama a Teresa. "¡Aló, Teresa! Tengo problemas con la tarea de matemáticas. Es muy difícil...." Después de hablar por dos horas Teresa le dice "Eres muy cómico, Ricardo".

> El jueves en el colegio Diego le da un presente a Teresa. Ella le dice "Muchas gracias. Eres muy generoso. ¿Sabes? Voy a la fiesta contigo".

> **Answer Key:**
> (1) una fiesta (2) amable (3) tenis (4) atlético (5) oye la radio

8. Collaborate with students in establishing a list of guide words. **Note:** Guide words are a brief list of difficult words or phrases that occur in the story. Display the guide words.

9. Have students practice with partners using only the story's illustrations (page 27) and the guide words (if needed).

10. Have volunteers tell the story to the class. Students may use illustrations and guide words, if necessary.

11. Assessment: Have students record the story on audiocassettes. Students may use **only** the illustrations. Guide words may be used by students who need more direction. Evaluate the cassettes and include them in students' portfolios.

12. Collaborate with students in writing the story based on the illustrations. Write the story as students copy it.

13. Have partners invent a new story or alter the original story. Have them draw new or altered illustrations and then tell the story to the class.

Step 1 | Gesturing New Vocabulary

Purpose: To introduce the new vocabulary.

1. Show the vocabulary list on the right, covering up the English and Gesture columns.

2. Introduce the first three words/ expressions.

3. Say the words one at a time and do the gestures.

4. Have students imitate the gestures silently.

5. Say the words and have students gesture with their eyes closed.

6. Test individual students randomly. Say a word and have students do the gesture. (If a word is not understood by several students, it must be included when teaching the following set of words.)

7. Do gestures and have students say the words.

8. Say the words and have students give the English equivalents.

9. Repeat this process (Steps 1-8) for the next set of three words until the vocabulary list is all presented.

10. Ask questions and have students answer.

   Sample Questions:
   ¿Quién es calvo en tu familia?
   ¿Estás triste o contento/a hoy?
   *¿Tienes un(a) hermano/a menor o
      mayor?*
   ¿Quién es cariñoso/a en tu familia?

11. The following day review the vocabulary list using the above steps with increased speed.

12. You may also want to check students' comprehension by creating matching quizzes and fill-in-the-blank exercises.

Note: Some ways to invent gestures include referencing American Sign Language books, making them up or soliciting student input.

Spanish	English	Gesture
la hermana menor	younger sister	Point to the family tree on page 134 in the textbook.
las fotos	pictures	Pretend to take pictures.
los abuelos	grandparents	Point to the family tree on page 134 in the textbook.
el abuelo	grandfather	Point to the family tree on page 134 in the textbook.
calvo	bald	Point to the head of a bald person.
la abuela	grandma	Point to the family tree on page 134 in the textbook.
el tío	uncle	Point to the family tree on page 134 in the textbook.
la prima	cousin (female)	Point to the family tree on page 134 in the textbook.
la hija única	only daughter	Point to the family tree on page 134 in the textbook.
el hermano mayor	older brother	Point to the family tree on page 134 in the textbook.
(él) canta	(he) sings	Mimic singing.
me gusta	I like	Point to yourself and show an item.
(yo) quiero	(I) want	Bring your hands towards your chest.
delgado	thin	Put your thumb and your index finger close together.
triste	sad	Make a sad face.
toda	everybody	Make circular motion pointing to everybody in class.
contenta	happy	Make a happy face.
cariñosa	caring	Pet an animal.

Additional Vocabulary

año, boda, conocerla, mientras, (él) escucha, consentida, finalmente, perro, mostrarme, ya, viajar, (la familia) abraza

Situations

1 Es el aniversario de bodas del **abuelo** y **la abuela** de Juan. En dos días hay una gran fiesta para sus **abuelos.** Cien personas van a ir a la fiesta. **Toda** la familia está muy **contenta.** Carlos, **el tío** de Juan, y su **prima,** Rosa, preparan la fiesta. María, **la hija única** de Carlos, hace un álbum de **fotos** de los abuelos como presente para ellos. La familia tiene otro presente muy grande que es secreto.

2 Mientras Carlos, Rosa y Juan preparan la fiesta, Graciela, **la hermana menor** de Juan y su **hermano mayor**, Alberto, juegan al béisbol en el patio de la casa. De repente la bola de béisbol da en el garaje. Graciela y Alberto van por la bola. Ellos ven un *(name of sports car)* rojo en el garaje. Graciela le dice a Alberto "¡Es el presente secreto para los abuelos! ¿Vamos a *(fast food restaurant)* en el carro nuevo? **¡Quiero** comer una hamburguesa!" Alberto responde "¡Sí, pero no digas nada!" Graciela dice "Sí, sí, Alberto. ¡Vamos!" Ellos van a *(fast food restaurant)*.

3 Después de una hora, Alberto y Graciela, retornan a la casa y "¡bumm!". Ellos destruyen la puerta del garaje con el carro nuevo. El abuelo oye y corre al garaje. Graciela está muy, muy **triste** y le dice al abuelo "Lo siento. El carro es tu presente secreto". Alberto también dice "Lo siento" y le **canta** "¡Feliz aniversario! al abuelo. Toda la familia va al garaje y grita "¡Ay, caramba!" El abuelo es muy **cariñoso** y dice "**Me gusta** el carro nuevo". La abuela le dice al abuelo "¡Eres **calvo, delgado** y alto! ¡Te vas a ver ridículo en ese carro rojo!" El abuelo le responde "Es nuestro presente y me gusta mucho". Los abuelos van a casa en su nuevo y rápido carro rojo.

Advanced Story

La familia de Patricia

Patricia es de España y estudia en los Estados Unidos por un año. Tiene un novio de Texas. Se llama David. Ellos van en avión a Madrid para la boda de su **hermana menor**, María. En el avión, Patricia y David miran **fotos** de la familia de Patricia. Patricia tiene una familia muy grande y David está nervioso de conocerla. David toma un refresco mientras escucha a Patricia hablar sobre su familia. "Aquí están mis **abuelos**. Mi **abuelo** se llama Héctor. Él es **calvo**. Mi **abuela** se llama María. Es muy generosa. Y aquí están mi **tío**, Alberto, y mi **prima**, Ángela. Ella es **hija única** y es muy consentida. También está aquí mi **hermano mayor**. Él **canta** en una banda. **Me gusta** mucho su música. La banda es muy popular en Madrid. Finalmente, aquí están mi hermana menor, mi madre y mi perro, Pepe. **Quiero** mucho a Pepe. Es **delgado,** adorable y nunca está **triste**."

"Gracias, Patricia, por mostrarme las fotos de tu familia. Ahora ya no estoy nervioso de conocer a tu familia" le dice David. Después de viajar diez horas en avión, llegan a Madrid. **Toda** la familia está en el aeropuerto. Patricia está muy **contenta**. La familia abraza y besa a Patricia y a David. David dice "¡Patricia, tienes una familia muy **cariñosa**!"

Purpose: To use the vocabulary to tell a story.

1. Display the vocabulary list (page 29) in class. Students use the list as a reference.

2. Show illustrations (page 31), then tell the story. Have students follow along.

3. Pick student actors for the story.

4. Tell the story in an animated way. At the same time help student actors perform the story.

5. Ask **Yes/No Questions**.

> ¿Tiene la hermana menor de Patricia una boda? (sí)
> ¿Se llama su abuelo Juan? (no)
> ¿Es Ángela la hija única de Alberto? (sí)
> ¿Está Pepe siempre triste? (no)
> ¿Es la familia de Patricia cariñosa? (sí)

6. Ask **Comprehension Questions** about the story.

¿Por qué van David y María a Madrid?	Ellos van para la boda de la hermana menor de Patricia.
¿Qué miran Patricia y David en el avión?	Ellos miran fotos de la familia de Patricia.
¿Qué hace el hermano mayor de Patricia?	Él canta en una banda.
¿Cómo es Pepe?	Pepe es delgado, adorable y nunca está triste.
¿Quién está en el aeropuerto?	Toda la familia de Patricia están el aeropuerto.

7. Read the **Changed Story** and have students correct it.

> Patricia es de España y estudia en los Estados Unidos por un año. Tiene un novio de Texas. Se llama David. Ellos van en avión a Madrid para la boda de su hermana menor, María. En el avión, Patricia y David miran (1) <u>amigos</u> de la familia de Patricia. Patricia tiene una familia muy grande, y David está nervioso de conocerla. David toma un refresco mientras escucha a Patricia hablar sobre su familia. "Aquí están (2) <u>mis padres</u>. Mi abuelo se llama Héctor. Él es (3) <u>guapo</u>. Mi abuela se llama María. Es muy generosa. Y aquí están mi tío, Alberto, y mi prima, Ángela. Ella es hija única y es muy consentida. También está aquí mi hermano mayor. Él (4) <u>baila</u> en una banda. Me gusta mucho su música. La banda es muy popular en Madrid. Finalmente, aquí están mi hermana menor, mi madre y mi perro, Pepe. Quiero a Pepe mucho. Es delgado, adorable y nunca está triste."

> "Gracias, Patricia, por mostrarme las fotos de tu familia. Ahora ya no estoy nervioso de conocer a tu familia" le dice David. Después de viajar diez horas en avión, llegan a Madrid. Toda la familia está en el aeropuerto. Patricia está muy (5) <u>nerviosa</u>. La familia abraza y besa a Patricia y a David. David dice "¡Patricia, tienes una familia muy cariñosa!"

> **Answer Key:**
> (1) fotos (2) mis abuelos (3) calvo (4) canta (5) contenta

8. Collaborate with students in establishing a list of guide words. **Note:** Guide words are a brief list of difficult words or phrases that occur in the story. Display the guide words.

9. Have students practice with partners using only the story's illustrations (page 31) and the guide words (if needed).

10. Have volunteers tell the story to the class. Students may use illustrations and guide words, if necessary.

11. Assessment: Have students record the story on audiocassettes. Students may use **only** the illustrations. Guide words may be used by students who need more direction. Evaluate the cassettes and include them in students' portfolios.

12. Collaborate with students in writing the story based on the illustrations. Write the story as students copy it.

13. Have partners invent a new story or alter the original story. Have them draw new or altered illustrations and then tell the story to the class.

Step 1 | Gesturing New Vocabulary

Purpose: To introduce the new vocabulary.

1. Show the vocabulary list on the right, covering up the English and Gesture columns.

2. Introduce the first three words/ expressions.

3. Say the words one at a time and do the gestures.

4. Have students imitate the gestures silently.

5. Say the words and have students gesture with their eyes closed.

6. Test individual students randomly. Say a word and have students do the gesture. (If a word is not understood by several students, it must be included when teaching the following set of words.)

7. Do gestures and have students say the words.

8. Say the words and have students give the English equivalents.

9. Repeat this process (Steps 1-8) for the next set of three words until the vocabulary list is all presented.

10. Ask questions and have students answer.

   Sample Questions:
   ¿Cuándo es tu cumpleaños?
   ¿Te gustan las sorpresas?
   ¿Cómo se llama tu canción favorita?
   ¿Quieres tener mucho dinero?
   ¿Puedes cantar bien?

11. The following day review the vocabulary list using the above steps with increased speed.

12. You may also want to check students' comprehension by creating matching quizzes and fill-in-the-blank exercises.

Note: Some ways to invent gestures include referencing American Sign Language books, making them up or soliciting student input.

Spanish	English	Gesture
junio	June	Point to the month of June in a calendar.
el cumpleaños	birthday	Say the date of your birthday.
todos	everybody	Point to everybody.
(ellos) vienen	(they) come	Gesture for a student to come to you.
la sorpresa	surprise	Look surprised.
(ella) abre	(she) opens	Open the door.
(ellos) entran	(they) enter	Enter the classroom.
la caja	box	Draw a box in the air.
¡Feliz cumpleaños!	Happy Birthday!	Sing Happy Birthday.
(él) salta	(he) jumps	Jump.
la canción	song	Say the name of a popular song.
tan	so	Point to a student and say *Es tan alto.*
el disco compacto	compact disc	Point to a CD.
(tú) puedes	(you) can	Gesture rooting for someone.
el dinero	money	Rub your fore finger and thumb together.
miles	millions	Draw a million dollar bill.
todos los días	every day	Point to all the days of a month on a calendar.

Situations

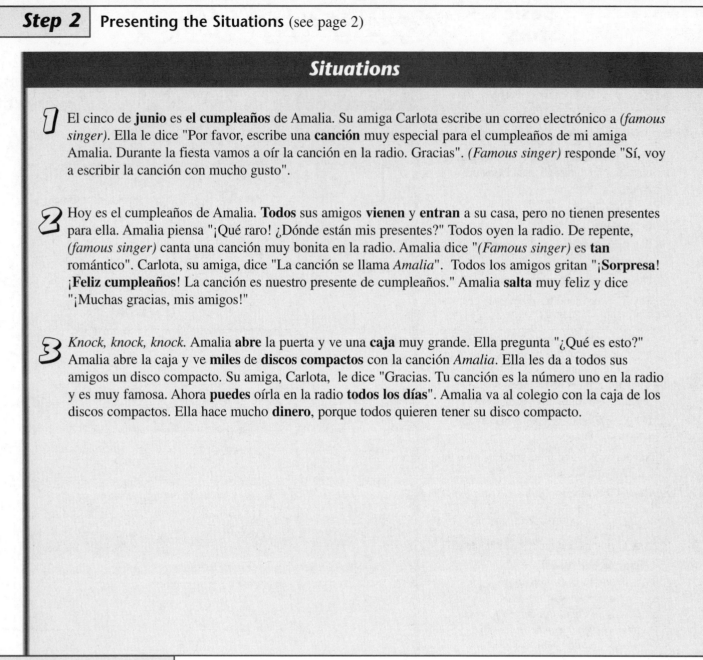

1 El cinco de **junio** es **el cumpleaños** de Amalia. Su amiga Carlota escribe un correo electrónico a *(famous singer)*. Ella le dice "Por favor, escribe una **canción** muy especial para el cumpleaños de mi amiga Amalia. Durante la fiesta vamos a oír la canción en la radio. Gracias". *(Famous singer)* responde "Sí, voy a escribir la canción con mucho gusto".

2 Hoy es el cumpleaños de Amalia. **Todos** sus amigos **vienen** y **entran** a su casa, pero no tienen presentes para ella. Amalia piensa "¡Qué raro! ¿Dónde están mis presentes?" Todos oyen la radio. De repente, *(famous singer)* canta una canción muy bonita en la radio. Amalia dice "*(Famous singer)* es **tan** romántico". Carlota, su amiga, dice "La canción se llama *Amalia*". Todos los amigos gritan "¡**Sorpresa**! ¡**Feliz cumpleaños**! La canción es nuestro presente de cumpleaños." Amalia **salta** muy feliz y dice "¡Muchas gracias, mis amigos!"

3 *Knock, knock, knock.* Amalia **abre** la puerta y ve una **caja** muy grande. Ella pregunta "¿Qué es esto?" Amalia abre la caja y ve **miles** de **discos compactos** con la canción *Amalia*. Ella les da a todos sus amigos un disco compacto. Su amiga, Carlota, le dice "Gracias. Tu canción es la número uno en la radio y es muy famosa. Ahora **puedes** oírla en la radio **todos los días**". Amalia va al colegio con la caja de los discos compactos. Ella hace mucho **dinero**, porque todos quieren tener su disco compacto.

Basic Story

Una sorpresa grande

Hoy es el diecinueve de **junio** y es **el cumpleaños** de Margarita. **Todos** sus amigos **vienen** a su casa para su fiesta de cumpleaños. Sus amigos tienen una **sorpresa** muy grande para ella. Su amiga, Alicia, **abre** la puerta de la casa. Cuatro chicos **entran** a la casa con una **caja** enorme. Los chicos gritan "¡**Feliz cumpleaños**, Margarita!" y el grupo de música favorito de Margarita **salta** de la caja y le canta *(name of birthday song)*. Margarita está muy, muy feliz. Ella toma el micrófono y canta su **canción** favorita, *(name of popular song)*. El grupo de música está muy contento y dice "¡Qué cantante **tan** fantástica!" "Gracias" dice Margarita. "¿Quieres ser nuestra cantante? Hacemos un nuevo **disco compacto**. **Puedes** ganar mucho **dinero**, posiblemente **miles** de dólares." Margarita responde "¡Sí! ¡Sí! **Todos los días** digo que quiero ser una cantante famosa". La fiesta continua y todos bailan y cantan con Margarita.

Purpose: To use the vocabulary to tell a story.

1. Display the vocabulary list (page 33) in class. Students use the list as a reference.

2. Show illustrations (page 35), then tell the story. Have students follow along.

3. Pick student actors for the story.

4. Tell the story in an animated way. At the same time help student actors perform the story.

5. Ask **Yes/No Questions**.

> ¿Es hoy el cumpleaños de Margarita? (sí)
> ¿Entran tres chicas con una caja enorme? (no)
> ¿Salta su madre de la caja? (no)
> ¿Canta Margarita su canción favorita? (sí)
> ¿Puede Margarita hacer mucho dinero? (sí)

6. Ask **Comprehension Questions** about the story.

> ¿Qué día es el cumpleaños de Margarita?   Su cumpleaños es el diecinueve de junio.
> ¿Quién vienen a su casa para su fiesta?   Todos sus amigos vienen a su casa para su fiesta.
> ¿Qué gritan los chicos?   Ellos gritan "¡Feliz cumpleaños, Margarita!"
> ¿Qué hace el grupo de música?   Ellos hacen un nuevo disco compacto.
> ¿Cuánto dinero puede hacer Margarita?   Ella puede hacer miles de dólares.

7. Read the **Changed Story** and have students correct it.

> Hoy es el diecinueve de (1) <u>mayo</u> y es el cumpleaños de Margarita. Todos sus amigos (2) <u>salen</u> a su casa para su fiesta de cumpleaños. Sus amigos tienen una sorpresa muy grande para ella. Su amiga, Alicia, abre la puerta de la casa. Cuatro chicos entran a la casa con una caja enorme. Los chicos gritan "¡(3) <u>Tanto gusto</u>, Margarita!" y el grupo de música favorito de Margarita salta de la caja y le canta (*name of birthday song*). Margarita está muy, muy feliz. Ella toma el micrófono y canta su canción favorita, (*name of popular song*). El grupo de música está muy contento y dice "¡Qué cantante tan fantástica!" "Gracias" dice Margarita. "¿Quieres ser nuestra cantante? Hacemos un nuevo (4) <u>libro</u>. Puedes hacer mucho dinero, posiblemente miles de dólares." Margarita responde "¡Sí! ¡Sí! (5) <u>Nunca</u> digo que quiero ser una cantante famosa". La fiesta continua y todos bailan y cantan con Margarita.

> **Answer Key:**
> (1) junio (2) vienen (3) Feliz cumpleaños (4) disco compacto (5) Todos los días

8. Collaborate with students in establishing a list of guide words. **Note:** Guide words are a brief list of difficult words or phrases that occur in the story. Display the guide words.

9. Have students practice with partners using only the story's illustrations (page 35) and the guide words (if needed).

10. Have volunteers tell the story to the class. Students may use illustrations and guide words, if necessary.

11. Assessment: Have students record the story on audiocassettes. Students may use **only** the illustrations. Guide words may be used by students who need more direction. Evaluate the cassettes and include them in students' portfolios.

12. Collaborate with students in writing the story based on the illustrations. Write the story as students copy it.

13. Have partners invent a new story or alter the original story. Have them draw new or altered illustrations and then tell the story to the class.

Step 1 | Gesturing New Vocabulary

Purpose: To introduce the new vocabulary.

1. Show the vocabulary list on the right, covering up the English and Gesture columns.

2. Introduce the first three words/ expressions.

3. Say the words one at a time and do the gestures.

4. Have students imitate the gestures silently.

5. Say the words and have students gesture with their eyes closed.

6. Test individual students randomly. Say a word and have students do the gesture. (If a word is not understood by several students, it must be included when teaching the following set of words.)

7. Do gestures and have students say the words.

8. Say the words and have students give the English equivalents.

9. Repeat this process (Steps 1-8) for the next set of three words until the vocabulary list is all presented.

10. Ask questions and have students answer.

   Sample Questions:
   ¿Juegas al fútbol?
   ¿Tienes pelo negro o rubio?
   ¿Lloras mucho?
   ¿Montas en bicicleta?
   ¿Cuándo haces un viaje?

11. The following day review the vocabulary list using the above steps with increased speed.

12. You may also want to check students' comprehension by creating matching quizzes and fill-in-the-blank exercises.

Note: Some ways to invent gestures include referencing American Sign Language books, making them up or soliciting student input.

Spanish	English	Gesture
(ella) hace un viaje	(she) takes a trip	Hold a suitcase and walk.
la semana	week	Demonstrate on the calendar on page 200 in the textbook.
el fútbol	soccer	Kick a ball.
anteayer	the day before yesterday	Demonstrate on the calendar on page 200 in the textbook.
montar	to ride	Ride a horse.
la pelota	ball	Hold a ball.
rápidamente	quickly	Walk quickly.
buscar	to look for	Shield your eyes with a hand.
vieja	old	Say *la abuela*.
doscientos	two hundred	Write the number on the board.
soñar	to dream	Close your eyes and smile.
el pelo	hair	Point to your hair.
los ojos	eyes	Point to your eyes.
la guitarra	guitar	Strum a guitar.
quinientas	fifty hundred	Write the number on the board.
(ella) llora	(she) cries	Mimic crying.
pasar	to spend (time)	Tap a watch.

Additional Vocabulary
(ella) patea, mar, en vez, encontrar, (ella) encuentra, botella, quizás, (ella) se duerme, (ella) empieza, nombre, (ella) se despierta, alrededor

Situations

1 Clara y sus tres hijos van a *(fast food restaurant with a play area)*. Los hijos saltan en una caja grande con **doscientas pelotas**. Clara empieza a **soñar** al ver a sus hijos tan felices. De repente, Clara no puede ver a Juanito en la caja y está muy nerviosa. Clara salta **rápidamente** en la caja con pelotas y saca a Juanito de la caja del **pelo**. Clara mira su mano y grita "¡Ay, caramba! ¿Dónde está mi diamante? Es muy **viejo**. Es un diamante de **quinientos** años que era de mi abuela". La mamá **llora** y llora.

2 Juanito le dice a su mamá "No hay problema, mamá. Vamos a **buscar** tu diamante". Todos los niños saltan en la caja con pelotas y buscan el diamante. Hay un problema. Ellos no pueden abrir sus **ojos** entre la caja con pelotas. Solamente pueden buscar el diamante con sus manos. Ellos encuentran muchas cosas interesantes. Primero, encuentran una **guitarra**. Después, encuentran una pelota de **fútbol** y un reloj. Pero no encuentran el diamante de Clara. Ellos **pasan** muchas horas en *(fast food restaurant)*. De repente, el papá de Juanito llama por el teléfono celular y le dice a Clara "Una señora en *(name of store)* tiene tu diamante". Clara salta muy, muy feliz.

3 **Anteayer** Clara encontró su diamante. Clara está tan feliz que decide **hacer un viaje** con toda su familia a Santiago de Chile por una **semana**. Durante la semana, la familia **monta** a caballo y en bicicleta. También, juega al béisbol, al fútbol y al volibol en la playa. Clara y su familia están muy felices.

Advanced Story

El sueño de Anita

La familia Trujillo **hace un viaje** a Argentina por una **semana**. Hoy es lunes y ellos deciden ir a la playa. La hermana mayor, Anita, le dice a su hermano menor, Víctor, "Vamos a jugar al **fútbol**". Él le responde "¡Qué aburrido! **Anteayer** jugamos al fútbol. Yo voy a **montar** en bicicleta. ¡Adiós!" Anita, sus otros hermanos y sus padres juegan al fútbol. La madre patea **la pelota** y se va al mar. Anita corre **rápidamente** a **buscar** la pelota pero en vez de encontrar la pelota, encuentra una botella muy **vieja**, quizás tiene **doscientos** años. ¡Qué increíble! Anita quiere abrir la botella pero está muy cansada y se duerme en la playa. Anita empieza a **soñar**. Sueña que un chico guapo con **pelo** negro y **ojos** azules viene a por la botella. Él es muy romántico, toca **la guitarra** y canta una canción de amor. El chico se acerca a Anita y le da **quinientas** rosas rojas. Anita abre los brazos para besarlo. De repente, Anita oye a su madre. Ella grita su nombre "¡Anita, Anita!" Anita se despierta con sus brazos alrededor de su madre. Anita **llora** y dice "Quiero soñar y **pasar** más horas con el chico guapo".

Purpose: To use the vocabulary to tell a story.

1. Display the vocabulary list (page 37) in class. Students use the list as a reference.

2. Show illustrations (page 39), then tell the story. Have students follow along.

3. Pick student actors for the story.

4. Tell the story in an animated way. At the same time help student actors perform the story.

5. Ask **Yes/No Questions**.

   ¿Hace la familia Trujillo un viaja a España? (no)
   ¿Juega Anita al fútbol? (sí)
   ¿Encuentra Anita la pelota? (no)
   ¿Tiene el chico guapo pelo negro y ojos azules? (sí)
   ¿Le da el chico cuatro rosas a Anita? (no)

6. Ask **Comprehension Questions** about the story.

¿Qué hace la familia Trujillo?	Ellos hacen un viaje a Argentina.
¿Qué va a hacer Víctor?	Él va a montar en bicicleta.
¿Qué encuentra Anita?	Ella encuentra una botella muy vieja.
¿Cómo es el chico guapo?	Es muy romántico con pelo negro y ojos azules.
¿Qué toca el chico guapo?	Él toca la guitarra.

7. Read the **Changed Story** and have students correct it.

   La familia Trujillo hace un viaje a Argentina por (1) <u>un año</u>. Hoy es lunes y ellos deciden ir a la playa. La hermana mayor, Anita, le dice a su hermano menor, Víctor, "Vamos a jugar al (2) <u>tenis</u>". Él le responde "¡Qué aburrido! Anteayer jugamos al fútbol. Yo voy a montar en bicicleta. ¡Adiós!" Anita, sus otros hermanos y sus padres juegan al fútbol. La madre patea la pelota y se va al mar. Anita corre rápidamente a buscar la pelota pero vez de encontrar la pelota, encuentra una botella muy (3) <u>nueva</u>, quizás tiene doscientos años. ¡Qué increíble! Anita quiere abrir la botella pero está muy cansada y se duerme en la playa. Anita empieza a soñar. Sueña que un chico guapo con pelo negro y ojos azules viene por la botella. Él es muy romántico, toca la guitarra y canta una canción de amor. El chico se acerca a Anita y le da (4) <u>cincuenta</u> rosas rojas. Anita abre los brazos para besarlo. De repente, Anita oye a su madre. Ella grita su nombre "¡Anita, Anita!" Anita se despierta con sus brazos alrededor de su madre. Anita (5) <u>canta</u> y dice "Quiero soñar y pasar más horas con el chico guapo".

   Answer Key:
   (1) una semana (2) fútbol (3) vieja (4) quinientas (5) llora

8. Collaborate with students in establishing a list of guide words. **Note:** Guide words are a brief list of difficult words or phrases that occur in the story. Display the guide words.

9. Have students practice with partners using only the story's illustrations (page 39) and the guide words (if needed).

10. Have volunteers tell the story to the class. Students may use illustrations and guide words, if necessary.

11. Assessment: Have students record the story on audiocassettes. Students may use **only** the illustrations. Guide words may be used by students who need more direction. Evaluate the cassettes and include them in students' portfolios.

12. Collaborate with students in writing the story based on the illustrations. Write the story as students copy it.

13. Have partners invent a new story or alter the original story. Have them draw new or altered illustrations and then tell the story to the class.

Step 1 | Gesturing New Vocabulary

Purpose: To introduce the new vocabulary.

1. Show the vocabulary list on the right, covering up the English and Gesture columns.

2. Introduce the first three words/expressions.

3. Say the words one at a time and do the gestures.

4. Have students imitate the gestures silently.

5. Say the words and have students gesture with their eyes closed.

6. Test individual students randomly. Say a word and have students do the gesture. (If a word is not understood by several students, it must be included when teaching the following set of words.)

7. Do gestures and have students say the words.

8. Say the words and have students give the English equivalents.

9. Repeat this process (Steps 1-8) for the next set of three words until the vocabulary list is all presented.

10. Ask questions and have students answer.

   Sample Questions:
   ¿Cuándo come tu familia en el comedor?
   ¿Qué tienes en tu cocina?
   ¿Corres mucho?
   ¿Pones la mesa?
   ¿Te gusta la sopa?

11. The following day review the vocabulary list using the above steps with increased speed.

12. You may also want to check students' comprehension by creating matching quizzes and fill-in-the-blank exercises.

Note: Some ways to invent gestures include referencing American Sign Language books, making them up or soliciting student input.

Spanish	English	Gesture
el rey	king	Put a crown on a male student's head.
la reina	queen	Put a crown on a female student's head.
los invitados	guests	Point to the guests on page 205 in textbook.
(ellos) ponen la mesa	(they) set the table	Demonstrate setting a table.
el comedor	dining room	Point to the picture on page 227 in textbook.
las cucharas	spoons	Point to the picture on page 234 in textbook.
los cuchillos	knives	Point to the picture on page 234 in textbook.
los tenedores	forks	Point to the picture on page 234 in textbook.
los platos	plates	Point to the picture on page 234 in textbook.
las servilletas	napkins	Point to the picture on page 227 in textbook.
los vasos	glasses	Point to the picture on page 227 in textbook.
la cocina	kitchen	Point to the picture on page 226 in textbook.
la sopa	soup	Pretend to cool off a soup.
la pimienta	pepper	Turn a pepper mill and sneeze.
(él) corre	(he) runs	Run.
los cubiertos	silverware	Point to the picture on page 226 in textbook.
atrapar	to trap	Pretend to trap something in hand.
quemándose	burning	Gesture flames.
de prisa	hurry	Walk quickly and pant.

Situations

1. Hoy es el cumpleaños de Ramón. Los abuelos de Ramón y treinta **invitados** van a *(medieval arena)* para su fiesta de cumpleaños. Todos están en **el comedor**. Una chica **pone la mesa** con **platos** y **servilletas** solamente. La abuela le pregunta "Perdón, ¿no pones **cubiertos?**" La chica le responde "Estamos en el año mil uno y no hay **cucharas, cuchillos** o **tenedores**". La abuela dice "¡Qué problema para los chicos!"

2. La chica sirve primero **la sopa**. Los chicos toman la sopa con las manos. Ahora los suéteres de los chicos están sucios de sopa. La abuela le dice al abuelo "Ve a *(name of a supermarket)* y compra unos cubiertos plásticos. Los chicos necesitan cucharas. ¡**De prisa!**" El abuelo **corre** a *(name of a supermarket)* a comprar los cubiertos. Ahora la chica sirve el pudín. Los chicos toman el pudín también con las manos y empiezan a combatir con la comida. Ahora hay pudín, sopa, sal y **pimienta** por todo el piso. La chica sale de **la cocina** y grita "¡No! ¡No! ¡No!" El abuelo retorna del supermercado, pero ya es muy tarde. La abuela llora y le dice a la chica "Lo siento mucho".

3. Todos oyen la fanfarria. **El Rey** y **la Reina** salen a la arena. El Rey anuncia "El espectáculo va a empezar". Los caballeros montando en sus caballos salen a la arena. La competencia empieza. Un caballero tiene que **atrapar** a otro. Como hay pudín por todo el piso, los caballos caen sobre los invitados y sobre las mesas que tienen candelas y **vasos** de cristal. Un chico grita "¡La arena está **quemándose!**" El Rey dice "Salgan todos con calma". Ramón y sus invitados corren a sus carros. La abuela ve que todos los chicos están bien. Los abuelos están felices y dicen "¡Vamos a casa!"

Basic Story

Una gran fiesta

El Rey y **la Reina** de España preparan una gran fiesta para doscientos **invitados**. Veinte sirvientes **ponen la mesa** en **el comedor**. Unos ponen **las cucharas, los cuchillos** y **los tenedores**. Otros ponen **los platos, las servilletas** y **los vasos** de cristal. En **la cocina**, otros quince sirvientes preparan una **sopa** muy especial con mucha sal y **pimienta**. De repente, un muchacho **corre** por el comedor y toma todos **los cubiertos**. ¡Nadie sabe quién es! La Reina grita "¡Ah!" Todos los sirvientes corren para **atrapar** al muchacho. Después de una hora, lo atrapan. La Reina grita "¡La sopa está **quemándose** !" Los sirvientes corren a la cocina y gritan "¡Ay, caramba!" El Rey le grita a la Reina "¡Ya llegan todos los invitados! ¡**De prisa**! ¡Tenemos que comprar doscientas hamburguesas!"

Purpose: To use the vocabulary to tell a story.

1. Display the vocabulary list (page 41) in class. Students use the list as a reference.

2. Show illustrations (page 43), then tell the story. Have students follow along.

3. Pick student actors for the story.

4. Tell the story in an animated way. At the same time help student actors perform the story.

5. Ask **Yes/No Questions**.

   ¿Preparan el Rey y la Reina de España una gran fiesta? (sí)
   ¿Ponen tres sirvientes la mesa? (no)
   ¿Preparan los sirvientes la sopa en la cocina? (sí)
   ¿Toma el Rey todos los cubiertos? (no)
   ¿Está buena la sopa? (no)

6. Ask **Comprehension Questions** about the story.

¿Cuántos invitados vienen para la fiesta?	Doscientos invitados vienen para la fiesta.
¿Qué hacen veinte sirvientes?	Ellos ponen la mesa en el comedor.
¿Qué ponen los sirvientes en la mesa?	Ellos ponen las cucharas, los cuchillos, los tenedores, los platos, las servilletas y los vasos de cristal.
¿Qué toma un muchacho del comedor?	Toma todos los cubiertos.
¿Cuál es el problema con la sopa?	Está quemándose.

7. Read the **Changed Story** and have students correct it.

   El Rey y la Reina de España preparan una gran fiesta para doscientos (1) <u>chicos</u>. Veinte sirvientes ponen la mesa en (2) <u>la cocina</u>. Unos ponen las cucharas, los cuchillos y los tenedores. Otros ponen los platos, las servilletas y los vasos de cristal. En (3) <u>el comedor</u>, otros quince sirvientes preparan una sopa muy especial con mucha sal y pimienta. De repente, un muchacho (4) <u>camina</u> por el comedor y toma todos los cubiertos. ¡Nadie sabe quién es! La Reina grita "¡Ah!" Todos los sirvientes corren para (5) <u>gritar</u> al muchacho. Después de una hora, lo atrapan. La Reina grita "¡La sopa está quemándose !" Los sirvientes corren a la cocina y gritan "¡Ay, caramba!" El Rey le grita a la Reina "¡Ya llegan todos los invitados! ¡De prisa! ¡Tenemos que comprar doscientas hamburguesas!"

   Answer Key:
   (1) invitados (2) el comedor (3) la cocina (4) corre (5) atrapar

8. Collaborate with students in establishing a list of guide words. **Note:** Guide words are a brief list of difficult words or phrases that occur in the story. Display the guide words.

9. Have students practice with partners using only the story's illustrations (page 43) and the guide words (if needed).

10. Have volunteers tell the story to the class. Students may use illustrations and guide words, if necessary.

11. Assessment: Have students record the story on audiocassettes. Students may use **only** the illustrations. Guide words may be used by students who need more direction. Evaluate the cassettes and include them in students' portfolios.

12. Collaborate with students in writing the story based on the illustrations. Write the story as students copy it.

13. Have partners invent a new story or alter the original story. Have them draw new or altered illustrations and then tell the story to the class.

CAPÍTULO 6

Purpose: To introduce the new vocabulary.

1. Show the vocabulary list on the right, covering up the English and Gesture columns.

2. Introduce the first three words/ expressions.

3. Say the words one at a time and do the gestures.

4. Have students imitate the gestures silently.

5. Say the words and have students gesture with their eyes closed.

6. Test individual students randomly. Say a word and have students do the gesture. (If a word is not understood by several students, it must be included when teaching the following set of words.)

7. Do gestures and have students say the words.

8. Say the words and have students give the English equivalents.

9. Repeat this process (Steps 1-8) for the next set of three words until the vocabulary list is all presented.

10. Ask questions and have students answer.

   Sample Questions:
   ¿Cuándo viajas con tu familia?
   ¿Tienes hambre ahora?
   ¿Tienes escaleras en tu casa?
   ¿Sabes quién tiene una piscina en su casa?
   ¿Cuántas salas hay en tu casa?

11. The following day review the vocabulary list using the above steps with increased speed.

12. You may also want to check students' comprehension by creating matching quizzes and fill-in-the-blank exercises.

Note: Some ways to invent gestures include referencing American Sign Language books, making them up or soliciting student input.

Spanish	English	Gesture
(ellos) encienden	(they) light/turn on	Turn on a light.
las lámparas	lamps	Point to a lamp in the ceiling.
el aceite	oil	Pretend to pour oil and vinegar on a salad.
(ella) empieza	(she) starts	Stand next to a student and behind a starting line and start to race.
(ellos) viajaron	(they) traveled	Point over your shoulder and hold a suitcase.
al lado de	next to	Point to two students sitting next to each other.
Tengo hambre.	I am hungry.	Rub your stomach.
Tengo sed.	I am thirsty.	Hold your throat with your mouth open.
esta	this	Point to an item.
especial	special	Say the name of a special event (homecoming, pep rally, etc.).
por la noche	at night	Draw a moon.
las salas	rooms	Point to the classroom and gesture plural.
la planta baja	ground floor	Point to the picture on page 244 in the textbook.
los cuartos	bedrooms	Point to the picture on page 244 in the textbook.
el primer piso	first floor	Point to the picture on page 244 in the textbook.
las escaleras	stairs	Climb stairs.
¡Ayúdenme!	help me	Look terrified and scream.
la piscina	swimming pool	Draw a rectangle in the air and swim.
Tengo frío.	I am cold.	Shiver.

Additional Vocabulary

(ella) se sienta, cocineros, escondite, (ellos) se esconden, castillo, juego, nadie, auxilio, (él) rescata, haz (tú), toalla

Situations

1 Para las vacaciones de primavera Gilberto y Raúl **viajan** a Puerto Rico. Gilberto y Raúl hacen un crucero desde Puerto Rico hasta la Florida. Ellos están muy felices de ir en barco. El transatlántico es muy grande porque tiene muchas **salas**. Su **cuarto** está en **el primer piso**. El crucero **empieza por la noche.** Ellos **tienen hambre** y **sed** y, por eso, van al restaurante del barco. Allí comen mucha comida y toman muchos refrescos. Ahora ellos están muy cansados y sus estómagos están muy grandes.

2 Es de noche, Gilberto y Raúl se sientan **al lado de la piscina**. De repente, **las lámparas** se apagan. Gilberto y Raúl no pueden ver nada. Ellos oyen a una muchacha gritar "**¡Ayúdenme!**" El capitán grita "¡Hombre al agua!" Ellos ven a una muchacha en el océano. Gilberto y Raúl saltan al océano. El capitán pone un bote en el agua y los muchachos nadan con la muchacha al bote. El capitán **enciende** las lámparas de emergencia. Todos aplauden.

3 La muchacha dice "**Tengo frío**". Los muchachos caminan con ella hasta **las escaleras.** Ella va a **la planta baja** a su cuarto. Después de una hora, ella va al restaurante. Los chicos están allí y le dicen "¡Qué muchacha tan bonita!" Gilberto le pregunta "¿Tienes frío?" Ella le responde "No, estoy bien". Raúl le pregunta "¿Por qué te gusta nadar en el océano?" La chica le responde "Ja, ja, no me gusta. Me caí en el océano porque hay **aceite** en el suelo". Gilberto le dice "**Esta** *(pointing to her blouse)* es muy bonita". Ella le dice "Es para una noche muy **especial**. Ustedes son mis héroes". Ellos le preguntan a ella "¿Quieres bailar?" Ella les responde "Sí, con mucho gusto".

Advaced Story

El escondite

Los sirvientes **encienden las lámparas** de **aceite**. La fiesta **empieza**. Los invitados **viajaron** de toda Europa para venir a la fiesta. La Reina se sienta **al lado del** Rey y le dice "**Tengo hambre** y mucha **sed**. ¡Pásame una hamburguesa, por favor!" A los invitados la Reina les dice "**Esta** es una comida **especial** de nuestros cocineros". Todos los invitados gritan "¡Qué excelente comida!" El Rey les dice "Vamos a comer un poco de postre y, luego, vamos a jugar al escondite".

Por la noche todos los invitados juegan al escondite. Se esconden por todo el castillo: en **las salas** de **la planta baja**, en **los cuartos** del **primer piso** y en **las escaleras**. A las diez de la noche el Rey les dice "Tenemos que terminar el juego ya. ¿Dónde está la Reina?" Nadie sabe. El Rey grita "**¡Ayúdenme**, por favor a encontrarla!" Los sirvientes, los cocineros, los invitados y los perros buscan a la Reina. El Rey escucha algo "¡Ah! ¡Auxilio! ¡Auxilio!" El Rey y los perros corren a **la piscina**. La Reina está allí. El Rey no sabe qué hacer. No sabe nadar. De repente, el perro favorito de la Reina salta a la piscina y la rescata. La Reina besa a su perro y le dice al Rey "**Tengo frío**. ¡Haz algo! Pásame una toalla".

Purpose: To use the vocabulary to tell a story.

1. Display the vocabulary list (page 45) in class. Students use the list as a reference.

2. Show illustrations (page 47), then tell the story. Have students follow along.

3. Pick student actors for the story.

4. Tell the story in an animated way. At the same time help student actors perform the story.

5. Ask **Yes/No Questions**.

   ¿Encienden los sirvientes las lámparas de aceite? (sí)
   ¿Juegan los invitados al escondite por la noche? (sí)
   ¿Se esconden los invitados en las salas de la planta baja? (sí)
   ¿Corre la Reina a la piscina? (no)
   ¿Tiene la Reina calor? (no)

6. Ask **Comprehension Questions** about the story.

¿Qué encienden los sirvientes?	Encienden las lámparas de aceite.
¿De dónde viajaron los invitados?	Ellos viajaron de toda Europa.
¿Qué comen los invitados antes de jugar al escondite?	Comen un poco de postre.
¿Cuándo juegan ellos al escondite?	Ellos juegan por la noche.
¿Dónde se esconden los invitados?	Se esconden por todo el castillo: en las salas de la planta baja, en los cuartos del primer piso y en las escaleras.

7. Read the **Changed Story** and have students correct it.

   Los sirvientes encienden las lámparas de aceite. La fiesta (1) <u>termina</u>. Los invitados viajaron de toda Europa para venir a la fiesta. La Reina se sienta al lado del Rey y le dice "(2) <u>Estoy muy bien.</u> ¡Pásame una hamburguesa, por favor!" A los invitados la Reina les dice "Esta es una comida especial de nuestros cocineros". Todos los invitados gritan "¡Qué excelente comida!" El Rey les dice "Vamos a comer un poco de postre y, luego, vamos a jugar al escondite".

   (3) <u>De mañana</u> todos los invitados juegan al escondite. Se esconden por todo el castillo: en las salas de la planta baja, en los cuartos del primer piso y en las escaleras. A las diez de la noche el Rey les dice "Tenemos que terminar el juego ya. ¿Dónde está la Reina?" Nadie sabe. El Rey grita "¡Ayúdenme, por favor a encontrarla!" Los sirvientes, los cocineros, los invitados y los perros buscan a la Reina. El Rey escucha algo "¡Ah! ¡Auxilio! ¡Auxilio!" El Rey y los perros corren a (4) <u>la casa</u>. La Reina está allí. El Rey no sabe qué hacer. No sabe nadar. De repente, el perro favorito de la Reina salta a la piscina y la rescata. La Reina besa a su perro y le dice al Rey "(5) <u>Estoy nerviosa.</u> ¡Haz algo! Pásame una toalla".

   Answer Key:
   (1) empieza (2) Tengo hambre y mucha sed. (3) Por la noche (4) la piscina (5) Tengo frío.

8. Collaborate with students in establishing a list of guide words. **Note:** Guide words are a brief list of difficult words or phrases that occur in the story. Display the guide words.

9. Have students practice with partners using only the story's illustrations (page 47) and the guide words (if needed).

10. Have volunteers tell the story to the class. Students may use illustrations and guide words, if necessary.

11. Assessment: Have students record the story on audiocassettes. Students may use **only** the illustrations. Guide words may be used by students who need more direction. Evaluate the cassettes and include them in students' portfolios.

12. Collaborate with students in writing the story based on the illustrations. Write the story as students copy it.

13. Have partners invent a new story or alter the original story. Have them draw new or altered illustrations and then tell the story to the class.

Step 1 | Gesturing New Vocabulary

Purpose: To introduce the new vocabulary.

1. Show the vocabulary list on the right, covering up the English and Gesture columns.

2. Introduce the first three words/ expressions.

3. Say the words one at a time and do the gestures.

4. Have students imitate the gestures silently.

5. Say the words and have students gesture with their eyes closed.

6. Test individual students randomly. Say a word and have students do the gesture. (If a word is not understood by several students, it must be included when teaching the following set of words.)

7. Do gestures and have students say the words.

8. Say the words and have students give the English equivalents.

9. Repeat this process (Steps 1-8) for the next set of three words until the vocabulary list is all presented.

10. Ask questions and have students answer.

   Sample Questions:
   ¿Te gusta el invierno?
   ¿Dónde esquías?
   ¿Juegas al ajedrez o las maquinitas?
   ¿Qué haces por la noche?
   ¿Envías e-mails a tus amigos/as?

11. The following day review the vocabulary list using the above steps with increased speed.

12. You may also want to check students' comprehension by creating matching quizzes and fill-in-the-blank exercises.

Note: Some ways to invent gestures include referencing American Sign Language books, making them up or soliciting student input.

Spanish	English	Gesture
espera	(he) waits	Hold your hand up like you are stopping some one and point at a male student.
Hace buen tiempo.	It is nice weather.	Point outside and give a thumbs up.
Hace...grados.	It is...degrees.	Point to a thermostat.
Hace mucho sol.	It is very sunny.	Put on sun glasses.
Está nublado.	It is cloudy.	Draw clouds on the blackboard.
el básquetbol	basketball	Hold a basketball.
el basquetbolista	basketball player	Dribble a ball.
¿Qué tiempo hace?	What is the weather like?	Shrug your shoulders and point outside.
(él) envía	(he) sends	Put a letter in the mailbox.
el invierno	winter	Say *diciembre, enero, febrero.*
Está nevando.	It is snowing.	Point outside and gesture snow falling.
la nieve	snow	Gesture snow falling.
esquiar	to ski	Gesture skiing.
patinar sobre hielo	to ice skate	Demonstrate ice skating.
el ajedrez	chess	Pretend to move chess pieces.
por la noche	at night	Point to a clock and gesture sleeping.
los videojuegos	video games	Pretend to move a joystick in your hand.
afuera	outside	Point outside.

Situations

1 Gloria y Francisco salen de clases. Son las dos y media de la tarde y **hace buen tiempo**. **Hace** veinte **grados**. Gloria quiere jugar al **básquetbol.** Ella es una buena **basquetbolista.** Gloria le pregunta a Francisco "¿Vamos a jugar al básquetbol?" Francisco le responde "¡No tengo tiempo! Tengo que ir a casa y mirar la televisión. El hombre que presenta el tiempo en el canal cuatro es muy divertido. Es un espectáculo magnífico. ¡Ven conmigo a mi casa!"

2 Gloria y Francisco corren a su casa. Toda la familia de Francisco está en la sala. **Esperan** el reporte del tiempo del Sr. Chiste en la televisión. Sale el Sr. Chiste y grita "¿**Qué tiempo hace**?" De repente, vemos que el Sr. Chiste **esquía** a cien millas por hora en las montañas sin control porque **está nevando** mucho y no puede ver. Él colisiona con un hombre de **nieve,** pasa sobre una casa y, luego, da un salto mortal y termina de cabeza en la nieve. Toda la familia aplaude. El Sr. Chiste grita "¡Ay, caramba! **Patinar sobre hielo** es más divertido para mí. **El invierno** en Utah es una buena experiencia. ¡Hasta mañana!" Gloria dice "Quiero ver otra vez al Sr. Chiste mañana. Me gusta mucho".

3 Al día siguiente toda la familia de Francisco se sientan otra vez en la sala a mirar al Sr. Chiste. El Sr. Chiste dice "**Por la noche** va a **estar nublado**, pero no hay problema porque mañana va a **hacer mucho sol** en el día. Hoy no quiero estar **afuera**. Hoy quiero jugar al **ajedrez** con un amigo". El Sr. Chiste llama a su amigo Eduardo y le dice "Tengo un nuevo juego de ajedrez. ¿Quieres jugar?" Eduardo le responde "Sí, voy para allá". El Sr. Chiste y Eduardo juegan al ajedrez. Después de dos minutos de jugar no les gusta el nuevo juego de ajedrez. El Sr. Chiste grita "¡Costó mil de dólares! Voy a regresar este juego a la tienda. Mañana lo **envío**". Ellos entonces juegan a **los videojuegos** toda la noche. La familia de Francisco está muy contenta y juega también a las maquinitas.

Basic Story | ### Tiempos diferentes en hemisferios diferentes

Diego corre a su casa porque **espera** un e-mail de Enrique, su nuevo amigo de Arica, Chile. Diego abre la puerta de su casa y corre a encender la computadora. Diego lee el e-mail de Enrique.

A: Diego
De: Enrique

¡Hola, Diego! Es el diez de enero. Es verano y **hace buen tiempo**. **Hace** veintiocho **grados**. **Hace mucho sol** y no **está nublado**. Esta tarde voy a jugar al **básquetbol** con mis amigos. ¿Eres **basquetbolista**? Mañana voy a la playa a jugar al voleibol. ¿**Qué tiempo hace** en Colorado?

Enrique le responde a Diego y le **envía** un e-mail.

A: Enrique
De: Diego

¡Hola, Enrique! ¿Verano? ¿Estás loco? Es **invierno** y hace mucho frío. **Está nevando** y mis amigos y yo vamos a jugar al fútbol americano en **la nieve**. Mañana voy a **esquiar** y a **patinar sobre hielo**. Después de esquiar voy a jugar al **ajedrez** y **por la noche** juego a **los videojuegos**. ¡No es posible jugar al voleibol y al básquetbol **afuera**!

Diego le responde a Enrique.

A: Diego
De: Enrique

Diego, estás equivocado. ¡Vivo en el hemisferio sur y aquí es verano! Hace veintiocho grados centígrados.

Purpose: To use the vocabulary to tell a story.

1. Display the vocabulary list (page 49) in class. Students use the list as a reference.

2. Show illustrations (page 51), then tell the story. Have students follow along.

3. Pick student actors for the story.

4. Tell the story in an animated way. At the same time help student actors perform the story.

5. Ask **Yes/No Questions**.

   ¿Espera Diego un libro? (no)
   ¿Es el ocho de enero? (no)
   ¿Va Diego a jugar al básquetbol? (sí)
   ¿Es invierno para Enrique? (sí)
   ¿Juega Enrique al básquetbol? (no)

6. Ask **Comprehension Questions** about the story.

¿Qué espera Diego?	Diego espera un e-mail de Enrique.
¿Qué tiempo hace en Chile?	Hace buen tiempo.
¿Qué hace Diego con sus amigos?	Ellos juegan al básquetbol.
¿Qué tiempo hace en Colorado?	Está nevando.
¿Qué hace Enrique mañana?	Mañana Enrique esquía, patina sobre hielo, juega al ajedrez y a los videojuegos.

7. Read the **Changed Story** and have students correct it.

   Diego corre a su casa porque (1) <u>tiene</u> un e-mail de Enrique, su nuevo amigo de Arica, Chile. Diego abre la puerta de su casa y corre a encender la computadora. Diego lee el e-mail de Enrique.

   > A: Diego
   > De: Enrique
   >
   > ¡Hola, Diego! Es el diez de enero. Es verano y (2) <u>está nublado</u>. Hace veintiocho grados. Hace mucho sol y no está nublado. Esta tarde voy a jugar al básquetbol con mis amigos. ¿Eres (3) <u>de Colorado</u>? Mañana voy a la playa a jugar al voleibol. ¿Qué tiempo hace en Colorado?

   Enrique le responde a Diego y le envía un e-mail.

   > A: Enrique
   > De: Diego
   >
   > ¡Hola, Enrique! ¿Verano? ¿Estás loco? Es (4) <u>primavera</u> y hace mucho frío. Está nevando y mis amigos y yo vamos a jugar al fútbol americano en la nieve. Mañana voy a esquiar y a patinar sobre hielo. Después de esquiar voy a jugar al ajedrez y por la noche juego a los videojuegos. ¡No es posible jugar al volibol y al básquetbol (5) <u>ahora</u>!

   Diego le responde a Enrique.

   > A: Diego
   > De: Enrique
   >
   > Diego, estás equivocado. ¡Vivo en el hemisferio sur y aquí es verano! Hace veintiocho grados centígrados.

   Answer Key:
   (1) espera (2) hace buen tiempo (3) basquetbolista (4) invierno (5) afuera

8. Collaborate with students in establishing a list of guide words. **Note:** Guide words are a brief list of difficult words or phrases that occur in the story. Display the guide words.

9. Have students practice with partners using only the story's illustrations (page 51) and the guide words (if needed).

10. Have volunteers tell the story to the class. Students may use illustrations and guide words, if necessary.

11. Assessment: Have students record the story on audiocassettes. Students may use **only** the illustrations. Guide words may be used by students who need more direction. Evaluate the cassettes and include them in students' portfolios.

12. Collaborate with students in writing the story based on the illustrations. Write the story as students copy it.

13. Have partners invent a new story or alter the original story. Have them draw new or altered illustrations and then tell the story to the class.

CAPÍTULO 7

Step 1 | Gesturing New Vocabulary

Purpose: To introduce the new vocabulary.

1. Show the vocabulary list on the right, covering up the English and Gesture columns.

2. Introduce the first three words/ expressions.

3. Say the words one at a time and do the gestures.

4. Have students imitate the gestures silently.

5. Say the words and have students gesture with their eyes closed.

6. Test individual students randomly. Say a word and have students do the gesture. (If a word is not understood by several students, it must be included when teaching the following set of words.)

7. Do gestures and have students say the words.

8. Say the words and have students give the English equivalents.

9. Repeat this process (Steps 1-8) for the next set of three words until the vocabulary list is all presented.

10. Ask questions and have students answer.

   Sample Questions:
   ¿Te gustan las telenovelas?
   ¿Qué haces esta noche?
   ¿Cuándo lloras?
   ¿Cuál es tu programa de televisión favorito?
   ¿Cuántas horas te gusta dormir?

11. The following day review the vocabulary list using the above steps with increased speed.

12. You may also want to check students' comprehension by creating matching quizzes and fill-in-the-blank exercises.

Note: Some ways to invent gestures include referencing American Sign Language books, making them up or soliciting student input.

Spanish	English	Gesture
la telenovela	soap opera	Say the name of a popular soap opera.
el novio	boyfriend	Point to a boy and touch your heart.
celoso	jealous	Point to a boyfriend and a girlfriend. The girlfriend goes to another boy and the boyfriend says "No!"
el pintor	painter	Demonstrate painting.
esta noche	tonight	Draw a crescent moon on the blackboard and write today's date.
el control remoto	remote control	Change channels on a remote control.
el programa	show	Say the name of a television show.
apaga	turn off	Switch off a light.
el televisor	television set	Point to a television set.
ahora mismo	right now	Point to your watch emphatically.
déjame	let me	Beg.
llorando	crying	Cry.
(yo) alquilo	(I) rent	Say *Alquilo un apartamento.*
(el apartamento) cuesta	(it) costs	Outline the dollar sign.
(tú) dibujas	(you) draw	Draw an object in the air or on the blackboard.
estupendo	excellent	Thumbs up.
dormir	to sleep	Sleep.
(ella) permite	(she) permits	Nod your head.
casi	almost	Put your thumb and forefinger close together.
todavía	still	Point to a clock and say *Todavía hay cinco minutos.*

Additional Vocabulary
se ve, escena, (tú) amas, (yo) amo, (ellos) siguen, pagarlo, algún, mujer, te amo

Situations

1 Sergio está mirando un **programa** muy interesante sobre **el pintor** Pablo Picasso en **el televisor** de la sala. Sergio estudia arte en la universidad y tiene mucho interés en aprender a **dibujar**. Su hermana, Mónica, toma **el control remoto** y cambia de canal porque en **casi** cinco minutos empieza su **telenovela** favorita.

2 Sergio le grita a Mónica "¿Qué haces?" Mónica le responde "Tengo que mirar mi telenovela favorita. **Esta noche** pasan un episodio muy especial. **El novio** de Carmen va a estar muy **celoso** porque Carmen va a besar a su amigo Eduardo". Sergio le dice "Las telenovelas son para adultos solamente".

3 Graciela, la mamá de los chicos, entra a la sala y le dice a Mónica "¡No te **permito** ver la telenovela, Mónica! Debes ir a **dormir ahora mismo**". Graciela **apaga** la televisión. Mónica **llora** y llora. Sergio le dice a su mamá "No me gusta cuando Mónica llora. Voy a **alquilar** un apartamento para vivir solo". La mamá le dice "¡No! ¡No! Un apartamento **cuesta** mucho dinero". Sergio le dice a la mamá "¡Entonces, **déjame** ver el programa de Pablo Picasso! **Todavía** lo están presentado". La mamá le dice "Sí, mi amor. Pablo Picasso es **estupendo**". Sergio enciende la televisión y mira el programa con su mamá.

Advanced Story

Vidas Nuevas

Gloria es una actriz joven y muy famosa en **la telenovela** *Vidas Nuevas*. Su **novio** se llama David y es muy **celoso**. Su novio en la telenovela es Mario. Es **pintor**. **Esta noche**, Gloria y David están mirando un episodio de la telenovela. Gloria tiene el **control remoto**. **El programa** empieza y se ve a Mario besando la mano de Gloria. A David no le gusta la escena y le dice a Gloria "¡Amas a Mario! No soy estúpido. **¡Apaga el televisor ahora mismo**!" Gloria le responde "Oh, David. Soy actriz. No amo a Mario. **Déjame** ver la telenovela". Ellos siguen mirando la telenovela. En la escena ven a Mario **llorando.** Gloria le pregunta "¿Por qué lloras?" Mario le responde "Porque no tengo dinero. **Alquilo** un apartamento que **cuesta** mucho y no puedo pagarlo". "Pero, mi amor, tú **dibujas** muy bien y algún día vas a ser un artista **estupendo**, como Pablo Picasso." (Cuando Gloria le dice a Mario "mi amor" David salta en su silla.) "¿Te doy dinero, mi amor?" le pregunta Gloria a Mario. "No, no. Prefiero trabajar toda la noche y no **dormir**." De repente, una mujer bonita entra al estudio de arte de Mario y dice "¡Qué dibujos tan bonitos! ¿Me **permite** ver los dibujos?" "Sí, claro." "Le doy un millón de dolares por todos los dibujos. ¿Es suficiente dinero?" "Es **casi** suficiente." La mujer no dice nada. Mario le dice a la mujer "Te amo". Gloria corre a Mario y le dice "Ya no eres mi novio. ¡Adiós!" Gloria apaga el televisor y mira a David en los ojos y le dice "**Todavía** eres el amor de mi vida".

Purpose: To use the vocabulary to tell a story.

1. Display the vocabulary list (page 53) in class. Students use the list as a reference.

2. Show illustrations (page 55), then tell the story. Have students follow along.

3. Pick student actors for the story.

4. Tell the story in an animated way. At the same time help student actors perform the story.

5. Ask **Yes/No Questions**.

> ¿Se llama David el novio de Gloria? (sí)
> ¿Es David poco celoso? (no)
> ¿Es Mario pintor? (sí)
> ¿Quiere David ver la telenovela? (no)
> ¿Dibuja bien Mario? (sí)

6. Ask **Comprehension Questions** about the story.

¿Cómo es David?	David es muy celoso.
¿Qué empieza?	El programa empieza.
¿Por qué llora Mario?	Porque no tiene dinero.
¿Qué le gusta a la mujer bonita?	A ella le gustan los dibujos de Mario.
¿Quién es el amor de la vida de Gloria?	El amor de su vida es David.

7. Read the **Changed Story** and have students correct it.

> Gloria es una actriz joven y muy famosa en la telenovela *Vidas Nuevas*. Su novio se llama David y es muy celoso. Su novio en la telenovela es Mario. Es pintor. Esta noche, Gloria y David están mirando un episodio de la telenovela. Gloria tiene el (1) <u>disco compacto</u>. El programa empieza y se ve a Mario besando la mano de Gloria. A David no le gusta la escena y le dice a Gloria "¡Amas a Mario! No soy estúpido. ¡(2) <u>Enciende</u> el televisor ahora mismo!" Gloria le responde "Oh, David. Soy actriz. No amo a Mario. Déjame ver la telenovela". Ellos siguen mirando la telenovela. En la escena ven a Mario llorando. Gloria le pregunta "¿Por qué lloras?" Mario le responde "Porque no tengo dinero. Alquilo un apartamento que cuesta mucho y no puedo pagarlo". "Pero, mi amor, tú dibujas muy bien y algún día vas a ser un artista (3) <u>celoso</u>, como Pablo Picasso." (Cuando Gloria le dice a Mario "mi amor" David salta en su silla.) "¿Te doy dinero, mi amor?" le pregunta Gloria a Mario. "No, no. Prefiero trabajar toda la noche y no dormir." De repente, una mujer bonita entra al estudio de arte de Mario y dice "¡Qué dibujos tan bonitos! ¿Me (4) <u>gusta</u> ver los dibujos?" "Sí, claro." "Le doy un millón de dolares por todos los dibujos. ¿Es suficiente dinero?" "Es casi suficiente." La mujer no dice nada. Mario le dice a la mujer "Te amo". Gloria corre a Mario y le dice "Ya no eres mi novio. ¡Adiós!" Gloria apaga el televisor y mira a David en los ojos y le dice "(5) <u>Casi </u>eres el amor de mi vida".

> **Answer Key:**
> (1) control remoto (2) Apaga (3) estupendo (4) permite (5) Todavía

8. Collaborate with students in establishing a list of guide words. **Note:** Guide words are a brief list of difficult words or phrases that occur in the story. Display the guide words.

9. Have students practice with partners using only the story's illustrations (page 55) and the guide words (if needed).

10. Have volunteers tell the story to the class. Students may use illustrations and guide words, if necessary.

11. Assessment: Have students record the story on audiocassettes. Students may use **only** the illustrations. Guide words may be used by students who need more direction. Evaluate the cassettes and include them in students' portfolios.

12. Collaborate with students in writing the story based on the illustrations. Write the story as students copy it.

13. Have partners invent a new story or alter the original story. Have them draw new or altered illustrations and then tell the story to the class.

Step 1	Gesturing New Vocabulary

Purpose: To introduce the new vocabulary.

1. Show the vocabulary list on the right, covering up the English and Gesture columns.

2. Introduce the first three words/ expressions.

3. Say the words one at a time and do the gestures.

4. Have students imitate the gestures silently.

5. Say the words and have students gesture with their eyes closed.

6. Test individual students randomly. Say a word and have students do the gesture. (If a word is not understood by several students, it must be included when teaching the following set of words.)

7. Do gestures and have students say the words.

8. Say the words and have students give the English equivalents.

9. Repeat this process (Steps 1-8) for the next set of three words until the vocabulary list is all presented.

10. Ask questions and have students answer.

   Sample Questions:
   ¿Qué sabes cocinar?
   ¿Cuál es tu receta favorita?
   ¿Dónde aprendiste esa receta?
   ¿Te gusta la cebolla?
   ¿Qué haces cuando la comida está quemada?

11. The following day review the vocabulary list using the above steps with increased speed.

12. You may also want to check students' comprehension by creating matching quizzes and fill-in-the-blank exercises.

Note: Some ways to invent gestures include referencing American Sign Language books, making them up or soliciting student input.

Spanish	English	Gesture
cocinar	to cook	Pretend to stir the contents of a pot.
(ella) aprendió	(she) learned	Point behind you, then point to your head.
la receta	recipe	Point to the recipe on page 341 in the textbook.
(ella) trabaja	(she) works	Pretend to shovel dirt.
la olla	pot	Hold a pot.
(ella) añade	(she) adds	Pretend to add something in to a pot.
las cebollas	onions	Pretend to cut an onion and cry.
las zanahorias	carrots	Pretend to chew on a carrot.
los guisantes	peas	Draw peas in a pod.
el arroz	rice	Point to the picture on page 338 in the textbook.
el chorizo	sausage	Draw links of sausages on the board.
(ella) prueba	(she) tries	Put something in your mouth and taste.
hace falta	is missing	Pretend a finger is missing.
(ella) olvida	(she) forgets	Look as if you are trying to remember something.
quemada	burned	Gesture fire flames and smoke.
tan buena como	as good as	Compare two students.
mejor	best	Hold up your index finger, point to your self and look proud.
el mundo	world	Point to a world globe.
(ella) sonríe	(she) smiles	Smile.

Situations

1 La clase de cocina tiene una competencia entre tres grupos de estudiantes. Ellos **aprenden** cómo **cocinar**. La profesora les dice a los estudiantes de los tres grupos "Ustedes tienen que inventar una **receta** nueva. Tienen tres días para **trabajar** en este proyecto".

2 Los grupos empiezan a trabajar en las recetas en forma muy reservada. Cada grupo tiene una mesa para trabajar en sus recetas. El primer grupo **añade** veinte **cebollas** a una **olla**. Todo el grupo llora mucho. El segundo grupo añade muchas **zanahorias**. Todo el grupo está de color zanahoria. El tercer grupo habla mucho y **olvida** la comida que tiene en la estufa. De repente, la alarma suena. La comida del tercer grupo está toda **quemada**.

3 Hoy es el día final de la competencia. El director del colegio, el profesor de matemáticas y la profesora de cocina van a escoger la **mejor** receta. Cada grupo tiene en una olla su receta original. El director **prueba** la receta del primer grupo. Es una sopa de **guisantes**, pero hay un problema. El director es alérgico a los guisantes y la receta tiene muchos guisantes. El director grita "¡Ay, caramba!" y corre al baño. La profesora de cocina prueba la receta del segundo grupo y dice "Tiene mucho **chorizo** y le **hace falta arroz**. ¿Dónde está el arroz?" El segundo grupo responde "¡Ay, caramba!" El tercer grupo no tiene comida porque está toda quemada. El profesor de matemáticas **sonríe** y dice "La sopa de guisantes es la mejor del **mundo**. Es **tan buena como** la de un restaurante".

Basic Story

Bien está lo que bien acaba

Verónica, una chica de Nueva York, visita a la familia Banderas en Málaga, España. Hoy es el cumpleaños del señor Banderas y esta noche hay una fiesta con muchos invitados. Verónica va a **cocinar** paella para la fiesta. Ella estuvo en una clase de cocina y **aprendió** una **receta** deliciosa para hacer paella. **Trabaja** todo el día. Prepara la paella en una **olla** grande. **Añade** muchas **cebollas**, tomates, **zanahorias** y **guisantes**. También, añade **arroz**, **chorizo** y pescado. Pone la paella en la estufa. Después de diez minutos, **prueba** la paella. "¿Qué le **hace falta**?" piensa Verónica. "¡Necesita algo más! Necesita más sal y pimienta." Verónica oye el teléfono. Es su novio de Nueva York. Ellos hablan por dos horas y Verónica **olvida** la paella. De repente, recuerda la paella y grita "¡Ah! ¡Olvidé la paella! ¡Qué desastre!" Ella deja el teléfono y mira la paella. La paella está toda **quemada** y los invitados llegan en diez minutos. Verónica corre al restaurante *Paella Club,* que está muy cerca de la casa, y compra una paella. Verónica llega a la casa con la paella nueva un minuto antes que los invitados. Los invitados comen la paella. La señora Banderas dice "¡La paella es **tan buena como** la del restaurante *Paella Club!*" El señor Banderas le responde "¡No! ¡No! Es la **mejor** del **mundo**. Verónica la preparó". Verónica **sonríe**.

Purpose: To use the vocabulary to tell a story.

1. Display the vocabulary list (page 57) in class. Students use the list as a reference.

2. Show illustrations (page 59), then tell the story. Have students follow along.

3. Pick student actors for the story.

4. Tell the story in an animated way. At the same time help student actors perform the story.

5. Ask **Yes/No Questions**.

> ¿Cocina Verónica una paella? (sí)
> ¿Trabaja Verónica por una hora? (no)
> ¿Añade Verónica jamón a la paella? (no)
> ¿Olvida Verónica la paella? (sí)
> ¿Sonríe Verónica? (sí)

6. Ask **Comprehension Questions** about the story.

> ¿Qué cocina Verónica para la fiesta?   Ella cocina una paella.
> ¿Dónde prepara Verónica la paella?   Ella prepara la paella en una olla grande.
> ¿Cómo está la paella después de que   Está toda quemada.
> Verónica habla por teléfono?
> ¿Qué piensa la señora Banderas sobre la paella?   Piensa que es tan buena como la del restaurante *Paella Club.*
> ¿Qué piensa el señor Banderas sobre la paella?   Piensa que es la mejor del mundo.

7. Read the **Changed Story** and have students correct it.

> Verónica, una chica de Nueva York, visita a la familia Banderas en Málaga, España. Hoy es el cumpleaños del señor Banderas y esta noche hay una fiesta con muchos invitados. Verónica va a cocinar paella para la fiesta. Ella estuvo en una clase de cocina y (1) <u>olvidó</u> una receta deliciosa para hacer paella. Trabaja todo el día. Prepara la paella en una olla grande. Añade muchas cebollas, tomates, zanahorias y guisantes. También, añade arroz, chorizo y pescado. Pone la paella en la estufa. Después de diez minutos, (2) <u>apaga</u> la paella. "¿Qué (3) <u>necesita</u>?" piensa Verónica. "¡Necesita algo más! Necesita más sal y pimienta." Verónica oye el teléfono. Es su novio de Nueva York. Ellos hablan por dos horas y Verónica olvida la paella. De repente, recuerda la paella y grita "¡Ah! ¡Olvidé la paella! ¡Qué desastre!" Ella deja el teléfono y mira la paella. La paella está toda (4) <u>fresca</u> y los invitados llegan en diez minutos. Verónica corre al restaurante *Paella Club,* que está muy cerca de la casa, y compra una paella. Verónica llega a la casa con la paella nueva un minuto antes de los invitados. Los invitados comen la paella. La señora Banderas dice "¡La paella es tan buena como la del restaurante *Paella Club!*" El señor Banderas le responde "¡No! ¡No! Es (5) <u>la peor de España</u>. Verónica la preparó". Verónica sonríe.

> **Answer Key:**
> (1) aprendió (2) prueba (3) le hace falta (4) quemada (5) la mejor del mundo

8. Collaborate with students in establishing a list of guide words. **Note:** Guide words are a brief list of difficult words or phrases that occur in the story. Display the guide words.

9. Have students practice with partners using only the story's illustrations (page 59) and the guide words (if needed).

10. Have volunteers tell the story to the class. Students may use illustrations and guide words, if necessary.

11. Assessment: Have students record the story on audiocassettes. Students may use **only** the illustrations. Guide words may be used by students who need more direction. Evaluate the cassettes and include them in students' portfolios.

12. Collaborate with students in writing the story based on the illustrations. Write the story as students copy it.

13. Have partners invent a new story or alter the original story. Have them draw new or altered illustrations and then tell the story to the class.

Step 1 | Gesturing New Vocabulary

Purpose: To introduce the new vocabulary.

1. Show the vocabulary list on the right, covering up the English and Gesture columns.

2. Introduce the first three words/expressions.

3. Say the words one at a time and do the gestures.

4. Have students imitate the gestures silently.

5. Say the words and have students gesture with their eyes closed.

6. Test individual students randomly. Say a word and have students do the gesture. (If a word is not understood by several students, it must be included when teaching the following set of words.)

7. Do gestures and have students say the words.

8. Say the words and have students give the English equivalents.

9. Repeat this process (Steps 1-8) for the next set of three words until the vocabulary list is all presented.

10. Ask questions and have students answer.

   Sample Questions:
   ¿Qué quehaceres tienes que hacer en tu casa?
   ¿Qué es mejor, sacar la basura o pasar la aspiradora?
   ¿Quién arregla tu cuarto?
   ¿Cómo es tu abrigo?
   ¿A quién admiras?

11. The following day review the vocabulary list using the above steps with increased speed.

12. You may also want to check students' comprehension by creating matching quizzes and fill-in-the-blank exercises.

Note: Some ways to invent gestures include referencing American Sign Language books, making them up or soliciting student input.

Spanish	English	Gesture
la gente	people	Point to the people in the classroom.
(yo) admiro	(I) admire	Admire yourself in the mirror.
el armario	locker	Point to a locker.
los quehaceres	chores	Make a sweeping motion and vacuum.
(yo) arreglé	(I) fixed	Point behind you. Pretend to hammer a nail.
(yo) pasé la aspiradora	(I) vacuumed	Point behind you. Vacuum.
(yo) saqué la basura	(I) took out the garbage	Point behind you. Hold your nose and take out the trash. Demonstrate with a garbage can.
(yo) limpié	(I) cleaned	Point behind you. Scrub.
el abrigo	coat	Point to a coat.
(yo) colgué	(I) hung	Point behind you. Hold up a clothes hanger.
la ropa	clothes	Point to clothes.
(tú) tocaste	(you) touched	Point behind you. Touch something with your hand.
casarte	to get married	Point to your wedding finger.
conmigo	with me	Hold hands and walk with a student.
la campana	bell	Make a bell sound.
quizás	maybe	Shrug your shoulders.

Additional Vocabulary
(la campana) suena

Situations

1 Víctor y Marta van a la fiesta de graduación del colegio en una limusina muy grande. Victor trata de ser muy caballero con Marta y corre a abrir la puerta de la limusina, pero a ella le dice "¡No! ¡No! Gracias" y ella le abre la puerta a él. Él quiere ayudar a **colgarle** su **abrigo**, pero ella le dice "¡No! Gracias" y ella le cuelga el abrigo a Víctor.

2 Víctor y Marta bailan en la fiesta de graduación. Hay mucha **gente** en la fiesta. Víctor está triste porque Marta no va a ir a la misma universidad que él. Víctor le dice a Marta "Te quiero y te **admiro** mucho. ¿Quieres **casarte conmigo**?" Marta oye **campanas** en su cabeza y le dice "¡Eres tan romántico!" Él **toca** su pelo románticamente. Marta piensa y le dice a Víctor "¡Espera un momento! Antes de casarme, tengo unas condiciones".

3 Víctor le pregunta a Marta "¿Qué quieres?" Marta le responde "Si quieres casarte conmigo tienes que prometer que vas a ayudar con todos **los quehaceres** de la casa: **pasar la aspiradora**, **limpiar** los pisos y las ventanas, colgar **la ropa, arreglar** los carros, **sacar la basura**...". Él le dice "Espera, espera. Voy a hacer eso y más, pero no voy a sacar la basura. Eso no me gusta". Ella le dice "¡Ah, no! Entonces **quizás** ya no vas a ser mi esposo". "¿Y por qué no?" pregunta Víctor. "Bueno, baila conmigo y mañana hablamos. Te veo en mi **armario** a las siete de la mañana".

Advanced Story

El trabajo ideal

Es el primer día de clases. Raquel y sus amigas Luisa y Susana hablan sobre el verano pasado. Luisa dice "Estuve con mucha **gente** en un concierto del grupo *(name of a band)*. ¡Fue fantástico! *(Name of band member)* es excelente". "Y tú, Raquel, ¿dónde estuviste en el verano?" pregunta Susana. "Pues, ustedes saben que yo **admiro** mucho a *(name of same band member as above)*, ¿no?" dice Raquel. Luisa responde "Sí, claro, tienes todas sus fotos y sus CDs en el **armario**". Raquel dice, "Bueno, en junio trabajé con su banda durante todo el verano. Estuve con *(name of band member)* todos los días". "¿Y qué pasó?" le pregunta Susana. Raquel le responde "Viajamos en autobús por todo los Estados Unidos. Hice los **quehaceres** en el autobús. **Arreglé** el autobús, **pasé la aspiradora**, **saqué la basura**. ¡Ah! y también **limpié** su **abrigo** y **colgué** su **ropa**". "¡Qué! ¿**Tocaste** su ropa?" grita Luisa. "Sí, sí. Y me dieron mil dólares cada día por hacer todo eso" responde Raquel. De repente, una limusina llega al colegio. *(Band member)* sale del auto, va adonde Raquel y le da un diamante muy grande. *(Band member)* le dice "Raquel, ¿quieres **casarte conmigo**? Te quiero mucho". Todas las chicas del colegio gritan. **La campana** suena y Raquel le dice "**Quizás** en cuatro años. Tengo clase. ¡Adiós!"

Purpose: To use the vocabulary to tell a story.

1. Display the vocabulary list (page 61) in class. Students use the list as a reference.

2. Show illustrations (page 63), then tell the story. Have students follow along.

3. Pick student actors for the story.

4. Tell the story in an animated way. At the same time help student actors perform the story.

5. Ask **Yes/No Questions**.

   ¿Admira Raquel a *(name of band member from story)*? (sí)
   ¿Tiene Raquel sus fotos y sus CDs en el baño? (no)
   ¿Hace Raquel todos los quehaceres en el autobús? (sí)
   ¿Toca Raquel la ropa de *(name of band member from story)*? (sí)
   ¿Quiere Raquel casarse con él ahora? (no)

6. Ask **Comprehension Questions** about the story.

¿Dónde están las fotos y los CDs?	Están en el armario.
¿Qué quehaceres hizo Raquel?	Arregló el autobús, pasó la aspiradora, sacó la basura, limpió su abrigo y colgó su ropa.
¿Qué tocó Raquel?	Raquel tocó la ropa de *(name of band member)*.
¿Qué le pregunta *(name of band member)* a Raquel?	Él le pregunta "¿Quieres casarte conmigo?"
¿Cuál es la respuesta de Raquel?	Ella le dice "Quizás en cuatro años".

7. Read the **Changed Story** and have students correct it.

   Es el primer día de clases. Raquel y sus amigas Luisa y Susana hablan sobre el verano pasado. Luisa dice "Estuve con (1) <u>mucho guisante</u> en un concierto del grupo *(name of a band)*. ¡Fue fantástico! *(Name of band member)* es excelente". "Y tú, Raquel, ¿dónde estuviste en el verano?" pregunta Susana. "Pues, ustedes saben que yo (2) <u>olvido</u> mucho a *(name of same band member as above)*, ¿no?" dice Raquel. Luisa responde "Sí, claro, tienes todas sus fotos y sus CDs en el armario". Raquel dice, "Bueno, en junio trabajé con su banda por todo el verano. Estuve con *(name of band member)* todos los días". "¿Y qué pasó?" le pregunta Susana. Raquel le responde "Viajamos en autobús por todo los Estados Unidos. Hice los (3) <u>quesos</u> en el autobús. Arreglé el autobús, pasé la aspiradora, saqué la basura. ¡Ah! y también limpié su abrigo y (4) <u>compré</u> su ropa". "¡Qué! ¿Tocaste su ropa?" grita Luisa. "Sí, sí. Y me dieron mil dólares cada día por hacer todo eso" responde Raquel. De repente, una limusina llega al colegio. *(Band member)* sale del auto, va adonde Raquel y le da un diamante muy grande. *(Band member)* le dice "Raquel, ¿quieres casarte conmigo? Te quiero mucho". Todas las chicas del colegio gritan. La (5) <u>cama</u> suena y Raquel le dice "Quizás en cuatro años. Tengo clase. ¡Adiós!"

   Answer Key:
   (1) mucha gente (2) admiro (3) quehaceres (4) colgué (5) campana

8. Collaborate with students in establishing a list of guide words. **Note:** Guide words are a brief list of difficult words or phrases that occur in the story. Display the guide words.

9. Have students practice with partners using only the story's illustrations (page 63) and the guide words (if needed).

10. Have volunteers tell the story to the class. Students may use illustrations and guide words, if necessary.

11. Assessment: Have students record the story on audiocassettes. Students may use **only** the illustrations. Guide words may be used by students who need more direction. Evaluate the cassettes and include them in students' portfolios.

12. Collaborate with students in writing the story based on the illustrations. Write the story as students copy it.

13. Have partners invent a new story or alter the original story. Have them draw new or altered illustrations and then tell the story to the class.

Basic Story

CAPÍTULO 9

Step 1	Gesturing New Vocabulary

Purpose: To introduce the new vocabulary.

1. Show the vocabulary list on the right, covering up the English and Gesture columns.

2. Introduce the first three words/ expressions.

3. Say the words one at a time and do the gestures.

4. Have students imitate the gestures silently.

5. Say the words and have students gesture with their eyes closed.

6. Test individual students randomly. Say a word and have students do the gesture. (If a word is not understood by several students, it must be included when teaching the following set of words.)

7. Do gestures and have students say the words.

8. Say the words and have students give the English equivalents.

9. Repeat this process (Steps 1-8) for the next set of three words until the vocabulary list is all presented.

10. Ask questions and have students answer.

   Sample Questions:
   ¿Qué ropa llevas hoy?
   ¿Qué es mejor en tu opinión, pagar a crédito o en efectivo?
   ¿Cuándo llevas pantalones de lana?
   ¿Cuándo llevas botas?
   ¿Cuál es tu centro comercial favorito y por qué?

11. The following day review the vocabulary list using the above steps with increased speed.

12. You may also want to check students' comprehension by creating matching quizzes and fill-in-the-blank exercises.

Note: Some ways to invent gestures include referencing American Sign Language books, making them up or soliciting student input.

Spanish	English	Gesture
el viaje	trip	Pretend to drive a car as you suggest different destinations.
(ellos) pagan	(they) pay	Take money from your wallet.
el centro comercial	shopping center	Say the name of a popular shopping center.
los hombres	men	Say the names of male teachers in the school.
los pantalones	pants	Point to pants.
el algodón	cotton	Point to a label on a t-shirt.
la lana	wool	Point to a label on a sweater.
las camisas	shirts	Point to shirts.
el traje de baño	swimming suit	Gesture swimming and point to clothes.
los guantes	gloves	Put on a glove.
las chaquetas	jackets	Put on a jacket.
las mujeres	woman	Say the names of female teachers in the school.
las botas	boots	Put on boots.
el impermeable	raincoat	Hold an umbrella and point to a coat.
la ropa interior	underwear	Point to the pictures on page 364 in the textbook.
en efectivo	in cash	Show some cash.
llevar	to wear	Point to clothes you are wearing.
bronceado	suntan	Point to the skin of a person with a suntan.
las gafas de sol	sun glasses	Put on sunglasses.

Situations

1. Yolanda y Rosa son buenas amigas. Es el fin del año escolar y ellas tienen sus vacaciones de verano. Yolanda va de vacaciones a Alaska porque sus tíos viven allí. Rosa va de vacaciones a Mallorca, España. Yolanda hace su maleta para su **viaje**. Primero, pone muchos **pantalones** de **lana**, tres **camisas** de **algodón**, una **chaqueta** de lana y **ropa interior**. Yolanda busca sus **guantes** nuevos. Ella no sabe dónde están. Ella le grita a su mamá "¡Mamá! ¿Sabes dónde están mis guantes nuevos?" La mamá le dice "Mira debajo de la cama". Yolanda mira debajo de la cama y allí están.

2. Yolanda no tiene **botas** para su viaje a Alaska. Yolanda llama a su amiga Rosa "¡Aló, Rosa! ¿Quieres ir al **centro comercial** conmigo? Necesito comprar unas botas para el viaje". Rosa le responde "Sí, yo también necesito comprar un **impermeable**, un **traje de baño** y tal vez unas **gafas de sol**". Yolanda le dice "¡Excelente! Pero, Rosa, no necesitas comprar un impermeable porque yo tengo uno y te lo puedo prestar". "Gracias, Yolanda. Entonces, vamos al centro comercial en una hora y media. ¡Adiós!" "¡Hasta pronto!"

3. Yolanda y Rosa van a *(name of mall)*. Primero, ellas van al departamento de **mujeres** para comprar un traje de baño. Rosa ve un bikini rojo y dice "¡Qué bonito!" "Sí, Rosa, está muy bonito pero, ¿te gusta **llevar** bikini?" "Sí, sí, me gusta mucho." Rosa compra el traje de baño y lo **paga en efectivo.** Las chicas van ahora al departamento de cosméticos. Rosa dice "¡Necesito comprar loción de **bronceado** porque no quiero ser quemada por el sol de Mallorca!" Rosa compra diez lociones de bronceado. Ahora Yolanda y Rosa buscan y buscan unas botas para Yolanda. Buscan en el departamento de mujeres y en el de **hombres**, pero no las encuentran. Es verano y ninguna tienda tiene botas de invierno. Finalmente, Rosa le dice a Yolanda "Yolanda, yo tengo botas en mi casa. Te las puedo prestar". "Rosa, muchas gracias, mi amiga".

Basic Story

Un viaje extraordinario

Carlos y Silvia son millonarios. Siempre van de vacaciones por todo el mundo: África, Asia, Europa, América del Sur. Ahora en las vacaciones están muy aburridos y quieren hacer algo muy, muy diferente y divertido. Ellos oyen que la NASA tiene un **viaje** extraordinario para dos personas para ir al nuevo planeta Gizmo. Carlos y Silvia **pagan** dos millones de dólares para ir en ese viaje. Los pilotos de la NASA les dicen "Salimos en dos horas". Carlos y Silvia corren al **centro comercial** para comprar ropa nueva. Ellos no saben cómo es el tiempo en el planeta Gizmo, entonces tienen que comprar ropa de todo tipo. Primero van al departamento de **hombres**. Carlos compra **pantalones** de **algodón** y de **lana**, **camisas** y un **traje de baño**. También, compra **guantes** y **chaquetas** para el invierno. Carlos paga su ropa a crédito. Ahora corren al departamento de **mujeres**. Silvia compra unas **botas**, un abrigo de lana, un **impermeable** y mucha **ropa interior.** También, compra suéteres de lana y un traje de baño. Silvia paga **en efectivo**. Ellos corren a la NASA, llevan cinco maletas. Después de diez días de viaje llegan al planeta Gizmo. Allí hace mucho calor y sólo pueden **llevar** sus trajes de baño. Como la gente de Gizmo no usa ropa Silvia y Carlos les dan a ellos las cinco maletas de ropa. La gente de Gizmo les dan a ellos loción de **bronceado** y **gafas de sol.** Silvia y Carlos vuelven al planeta con el mejor bronceado de toda la galaxia.

Un viaje extraordinario

Purpose: To use the vocabulary to tell a story.

1. Display the vocabulary list (page 65) in class. Students use the list as a reference.

2. Show illustrations (page 67), then tell the story. Have students follow along.

3. Pick student actors for the story.

4. Tell the story in an animated way. At the same time help student actors perform the story.

5. Ask **Yes/No Questions**.

> ¿Van Carlos y Silvia de viaje al planeta Gizmo? (sí)
> ¿Pagan ellos dos dólares por el viaje? (no)
> ¿Corren ellos a un restaurante? (no)
> ¿Compra Carlos unos pantalones, unas camisas y un traje de baño? (sí)
> ¿Compra Silvia unas botas, un impermeable y una ropa interior? (sí)

6. Ask **Comprehension Questions** about the story.

¿Para qué pagan Carlos y Silvia dos millones de dólares?	Para ir en un viaje al planeta Gizmo.
¿A dónde van Carlos y Silvia antes del viaje?	Van al centro comercial.
¿Qué compra Carlos?	Compra pantalones de algodón y de lana, camisas y un traje de baño.
¿Cómo paga Silvia su ropa?	La paga en efectivo.
¿Con qué vuelven ellos al planeta?	Vuelven con el mejor bronceado de toda la galaxia.

7. Read the **Changed Story** and have students correct it.

> Carlos y Silvia son millonarios. Siempre van de vacaciones por todo el mundo: África, Asia, Europa, América del Sur. Ahora en las vacaciones están muy aburridos y quieren hacer algo muy, muy diferente y divertido. Ellos oyen que la NASA tiene un (1) <u>restaurante</u> extraordinario para dos personas para ir al nuevo planeta Gizmo. Carlos y Silvia (2) <u>reciben</u> dos millones de dólares para ir en ese viaje. Los pilotos de la NASA les dicen "Salimos en dos horas". Carlos y Silvia corren al centro comercial para comprar ropa nueva. Ellos no saben cómo es el tiempo en el planeta Gizmo, entonces tienen que comprar ropa de todo tipo. Primero van al departamento de hombres. Carlos compra pantalones de algodón y de (3) <u>papel</u>, camisas y un traje de baño. También, compra guantes y chaquetas para el invierno. Carlos paga a crédito su ropa. Ahora corren al departamento de mujeres. Silvia compra unas botas, un abrigo de lana, un impermeable y mucha ropa interior. También, compra suéteres de lana y un traje de baño. Silvia paga (4) <u>en cambio</u>. Ellos corren a la NASA, llevan cinco maletas. Después de diez días de viaje llegan al planeta Gizmo. Allí hace mucho calor y sólo pueden llevar sus trajes de baño. Como la gente de Gizmo no usa ropa Silvia y Carlos les dan a ellos las cinco maletas de ropa. La gente de Gizmo les dan a ellos loción de bronceado y (5) <u>hace sol</u>. Silvia y Carlos vuelven al planeta con el mejor bronceado de toda la galaxia.

> **Answer Key:**
> (1) viaje (2) pagan (3) lana (4) en efectivo (5) gafas de sol

8. Collaborate with students in establishing a list of guide words. **Note:** Guide words are a brief list of difficult words or phrases that occur in the story. Display the guide words.

9. Have students practice with partners using only the story's illustrations (page 67) and the guide words (if needed).

10. Have volunteers tell the story to the class. Students may use illustrations and guide words, if necessary.

11. Assessment: Have students record the story on audiocassettes. Students may use **only** the illustrations. Guide words may be used by students who need more direction. Evaluate the cassettes and include them in students' portfolios.

12. Collaborate with students in writing the story based on the illustrations. Write the story as students copy it.

13. Have partners invent a new story or alter the original story. Have them draw new or altered illustrations and then tell the story to the class.

Step 1	**Gesturing New Vocabulary**

Purpose: To introduce the new vocabulary.

1. Show the vocabulary list on the right, covering up the English and Gesture columns.
2. Introduce the first three words/ expressions.
3. Say the words one at a time and do the gestures.
4. Have students imitate the gestures silently.
5. Say the words and have students gesture with their eyes closed.
6. Test individual students randomly. Say a word and have students do the gesture. (If a word is not understood by several students, it must be included when teaching the following set of words.)
7. Do gestures and have students say the words.
8. Say the words and have students give the English equivalents.
9. Repeat this process (Steps 1-8) for the next set of three words until the vocabulary list is all presented.
10. Ask questions and have students answer.

   Sample Questions:
   ¿Te gustan los desfiles de modas?
   ¿Por qué?
   ¿Cómo es tu vestido o tu traje favorito?
   ¿Qué llevas de ropa hoy?
   ¿Cuál es tu perfume favorito?
   ¿De qué color son tus zapatos?

11. The following day review the vocabulary list using the above steps with increased speed.
12. You may also want to check students' comprehension by creating matching quizzes and fill-in-the-blank exercises.

Note: Some ways to invent gestures include referencing American Sign Language books, making them up or soliciting student input.

Spanish	**English**	**Gesture**
el desfile de modas	fashion show	Pretend you are a model at a fashion show.
la blusa	blouse	Point to a girl's blouse.
la seda	silk	Point to a blouse and then rub your index finger and thumb together to indicate fine quality.
rosada	pink	Point to something pink.
la bufanda	scarf	Gesture that you have a scarf around your neck.
la falda	skirt	Point to a skirt.
larga	long	Gesture long.
el bolso	purse	Point to a purse.
los zapatos	shoes	Point to shoes.
la corbata	tie	Gesture a tie.
el sombrero	hat	Point to a hat.
le queda	fits	Outline the contour of a body.
el vestido de novia	wedding dress	Point to a picture of a wedding dress.
la pulsera	bracelet	Point to a bracelet.
hace juego	matches	Point to matching clothes items.
los aretes	earrings	Point to earrings.
el collar	necklace	Point to a necklace.
las perlas	pearls	Draw on the blackboard.
el perfume	perfume	Pretend to squirt on perfume.

Additional Vocabulary
comentarista, final, noten (Uds.), diseñados, (ella) se tropieza, (ella) se cae, (él) percibe, encantador, olor

Situations

1 Melanie va a casarse en Chicago durante el verano. Melanie y sus damas de honor van a un **desfile de modas** para mirar los diferentes tipos de ropa para su boda. Ella ve muchos estilos de **vestidos de novias**. El vestido de novia favorito de Melanie es uno muy elegante de **seda**. A las damas de honor les gusta una **falda larga**, una **blusa** y una **bufanda**. La falda y la blusa son **rosadas** y **hacen juego**.

2 Melanie y su novio, Troy, van de compras para comprar el resto de la ropa para la boda. Melanie tiene que comprar un **bolso** blanco y unos **zapatos** blancos. Troy necesita comprar una **corbata** y también busca un **sombrero** blanco. Troy ve muchos sombreros pero no le gustan. Después de media hora, encuentra un sombrero muy grande y lo compra. También él compra sombreros para todos sus amigos. Melanie le dice "**Te queda** bien, pero no vas a poder besarme si llevas el sombrero". Troy le dice "No hay problema. Me lo quito para besarte".

3 Melanie y Troy tienen mucha hambre y van a un restaurante. Ellos se sientan y Troy dice "Me gusta mucho tu **perfume**". Melanie le dice "Gracias, mi amor". Melanie quiere comer pescado y Troy quiere comer paella. Melanie va al baño un momento. Cuando ella regresa su pescado está en la mesa, pero tiene algo que no es normal. Melanie grita "¡Ay, caramba! Este pescado tiene un **collar** de **perlas** y una caja pequeña en su boca". Troy le dice "Son para ti. Abre la caja." Melanie abre la caja y encuentra unos **aretes** y una **pulsera** de perlas que hacen juego con el collar. Melanie le dice "Eres muy romántico. Muchas gracias. Te quiero mucho".

Advanced Story

Un desfile de modas

Mercedes y Esperanza son dos mujeres muy bellas. Julio es un hombre muy guapo. Ellos son modelos para la revista *(name of fashion magazine)* de Nueva York. Ellos están ahora en un **desfile de modas** en Madrid. Un desfile de modas es un evento muy grande donde muchas personas ricas y famosas van para ver lo nuevo en ropa. El comentarista anuncia a los modelos "Mercedes lleva una **blusa** de **seda rosada** con una **bufanda** y una **falda larga**. También lleva un **bolso** de material sintético de *(name of fashion designer)*. Gracias, Mercedes. Señores y señoras, aquí viene Julio. Él lleva un traje blanco, **zapatos** negros, **corbata** roja y un **sombrero** azul. Señoras, el traje **le queda** bien a Julio, ¿no? Gracias, Julio. Y ahora para nuestro gran final está Esperanza. Ella lleva un extraordinario **vestido de novia** de *(name of fashion designer)* de París. Por favor, noten los guantes largos y elegantes y **la pulsera** de diamantes que **hace juego** con **los aretes**. También, lleva **el collar** de **perlas** más espectacular de toda Europa y los zapatos **de tacón** más altos diseñados en todo el mundo. De repente, Esperanza se tropieza y se cae en lo brazos del Príncipe de Gales. El príncipe percibe el encantador olor del **perfume** de Esperanza y le dice "¿Me puedes dar tu autógrafo? Ella le responde "Sí, señor. Con mucho gusto". Todo el mundo aplaude.

Purpose: To use the vocabulary to tell a story.

1. Display the vocabulary list (page 69) in class. Students use the list as a reference.

2. Show illustrations (page 71), then tell the story. Have students follow along.

3. Pick student actors for the story.

4. Tell the story in an animated way. At the same time help student actors perform the story.

5. Ask **Yes/No Questions**.

¿Están Mercedes y Esperanza en un desfile de modas en París? (no)
¿Lleva Mercedes una blusa de seda rosada? (sí)
¿Tiene Mercedes un bolso de seda? (no)
¿Le queda bien el traje a Julio? (sí)
¿Hace juego la pulsera con los aretes que lleva Esperanza? (sí)

6. Ask **Comprehension Questions** about the story.

¿Por qué están Mercedes, Esperanza y Julio en Madrid?	Porque tienen un desfile de modas allí.
¿Qué lleva Mercedes?	Lleva una blusa de seda rosada con una bufanda, una falda larga y un bolso de material sintético.
¿Qué lleva Julio?	Lleva un traje blanco, unos zapatos negros, una corbata roja y un sombrero azul.
¿Qué lleva Esperanza?	Lleva un vestido de novia, unos guantes largos, una pulsera de diamantes, unos aretes, un collar de perlas y unos zapatos de tacón.
¿Qué pasa al final?	Esperanza se cae en los brazos del Príncipe de Gales.

7. Read the **Changed Story** and have students correct it.

Mercedes y Esperanza son dos mujeres muy bellas. Julio es un hombre muy guapo. Ellos son modelos para la revista *(name of fashion magazine)* de Nueva York. Ellos están ahora en (1) <u>un colegio</u> en Madrid. Un desfile de modas es un evento muy grande donde muchas personas ricas y famosas van para ver lo nuevo en ropa. El comentarista anuncia a los modelos "Mercedes lleva una blusa de seda rosada con una bufanda y una falda larga. También lleva (2) <u>una pulsera</u> de material sintético de *(name of fashion designer)*. Gracias, Mercedes. Señores y señoras, aquí viene Julio. Él lleva un traje blanco, (3) <u>botas rojas</u>, corbata roja y un sombrero azul. Señoras, el traje le queda bien a Julio, ¿no? Gracias, Julio. Y ahora para nuestro gran final está Esperanza. Ella lleva un extraordinario (4) <u>traje de baño</u> de *(name of fashion designer)* de París. Por favor, noten los guantes largos y elegantes y la pulsera de diamantes que hace juego con los aretes. También, lleva (5) <u>el bolso</u> de perlas más espectacular de toda Europa y los zapatos de tacón más altos diseñados en todo el mundo. De repente, Esperanza se tropieza y se cae en lo brazos del Príncipe de Gales. El príncipe percibe el encantador olor del perfume de Esperanza y le dice "¿Me puedes dar tu autógrafo? Ella le responde "Sí, señor. Con mucho gusto". Todo el mundo aplaude.

Answer Key:
(1) un desfile de modas (2) un bolso (3) zapatos negros (4) vestido de novia (5) el collar

8. Collaborate with students in establishing a list of guide words. **Note:** Guide words are a brief list of difficult words or phrases that occur in the story. Display the guide words.

9. Have students practice with partners using only the story's illustrations (page 71) and the guide words (if needed).

10. Have volunteers tell the story to the class. Students may use illustrations and guide words, if necessary.

11. Assessment: Have students record the story on audiocassettes. Students may use **only** the illustrations. Guide words may be used by students who need more direction. Evaluate the cassettes and include them in students' portfolios.

12. Collaborate with students in writing the story based on the illustrations. Write the story as students copy it.

13. Have partners invent a new story or alter the original story. Have them draw new or altered illustrations and then tell the story to the class.

	Spanish	English	Gesture

Step 1 | Gesturing New Vocabulary

Purpose: To introduce the new vocabulary.

1. Show the vocabulary list on the right, covering up the English and Gesture columns.

2. Introduce the first three words/ expressions.

3. Say the words one at a time and do the gestures.

4. Have students imitate the gestures silently.

5. Say the words and have students gesture with their eyes closed.

6. Test individual students randomly. Say a word and have students do the gesture. (If a word is not understood by several students, it must be included when teaching the following set of words.)

7. Do gestures and have students say the words.

8. Say the words and have students give the English equivalents.

9. Repeat this process (Steps 1-8) for the next set of three words until the vocabulary list is all presented.

10. Ask questions and have students answer.

   Sample Questions:
   ¿Por qué es importante para ti estudiar el español?
   ¿Vas a ferias de trabajo?
   ¿Quieres ser un(a) diplomático/a de carrera?
   ¿Te gustaría trabajar como agente de viajes?
   ¿Cuándo piensas solicitar un trabajo?

11. The following day review the vocabulary list using the above steps with increased speed.

12. You may also want to check students' comprehension by creating matching quizzes and fill-in-the-blank exercises.

Note: Some ways to invent gestures include referencing American Sign Language books, making them up or soliciting student input.

Spanish	English	Gesture
trabajoso	hard	Wipe sweat from your forehead with your hand as you pretend to work hard.
el puesto	booth	Draw a booth on the blackboard as you say *el puesto*.
las Naciones Unidas	United Nations	Say *Las Naciones Unidas están en Nueva York*.
la diplomática	foreign diplomat	Say the name of well-known foreign diplomat.
la carrera	career	Give examples of careers.
la traductora	translator	Demonstrate translating.
la agencia de viajes	travel agency	Say the name of a travel agency.
las oportunidades	opportunities	Say different opportunities students have in school.
el negocio	business	Give names of businesses.
el guía de turismo	travel guide	Hold a hand high in the air and wave.
el agente de viajes	travel agent	Point to a person as you say the name of a travel agency.
solicitar	to apply (for a job)	Draw a blank job application on the blackboard and begin to fill it out as you say *solicitar*.
el milagro	miracle	Give example of miracles as you say *¡Es un milagro!*

Situations

1 El Sr. Armstrong viaja a España en avión. Se sienta al lado de la ventana. Una mujer, la Sra. Peterson, se sienta al lado de él. Él le dice a ella "Buenas tardes, señora. Me llamo Jeff Armstrong". Ella le dice "Mucho gusto. Me llamo Lori Peterson". Ella escribe en su computadora. Él le pregunta "¿Hace Ud. un viaje de **negocios**?" "Sí, soy **agente de viajes** y planeo una excursión para mi **agencia de viajes**". "Muy interesante." "Sí" le dice la Sra. Peterson y sonríe.

2 La Sra. Peterson le pregunta al Sr. Armstrong "¿Cuál es su **carrera**?" El Sr. Armstrong le responde "Soy **diplomático** de **las Naciones Unidas** y trabajo en España". "¡Qué trabajo tan interesante! Ud. habla muy bien el español" le dice la Sra. Peterson. "La verdad es que no hablo muy bien. En Madrid tengo una **traductora**." Ella le dice "Oh, estaré en Madrid también". Él le dice "Si me llama, podemos salir a comer". El Sr. Armstrong le da su número de teléfono en Madrid. Los dos están contentos.

3 El Sr. Armstrong y la Sra. Peterson toman el almuerzo en el avión. El Sr. Armstrong le pregunta "¿Por qué decidió ser agente de viajes?" La Sra. Peterson le responde "Una vez fui a una feria de trabajo. Fui al **puesto** de una agencia de viajes y me dijeron 'Tenemos varias **oportunidades** pero tiene que hablar español.' El español fue muy **trabajoso** para mi en el colegio. Fue un **milagro** que no recibí una *F*. Entonces fue allí que vi que el español es importante en el mundo. Estudié mucho y recibí una *A* en la clase de español. Al terminar el colegio, **solicité** un trabajo en una agencia de viajes como **guía de turismo** y ahora estoy aquí". El Sr. Armstrong le dice "Qué bueno que escogió trabajar en una agencia de viajes y ahora puedo tener el gusto de hablar con Ud. en este viaje".

Basic Story

La feria de trabajo

Claudia y sus amigos están en la clase de español y le gritan al Sr. Gómez, su profesor de español, "El español es muy **trabajoso**. ¿Por qué es tan importante estudiar español?" El Sr. Gómez les responde "Porque va a ser muy importante para su futuro. Esta semana hay una feria de trabajo en el gimnasio. Como tarea ustedes tienen que ir a esa feria y aprender por qué el español es importante en el mundo".

Después del colegio, Claudia y sus amigos van a la feria de trabajo. Primero, van al **puesto** de **las Naciones Unidas**. Claudia le pregunta a una mujer que está en el puesto "¿Por qué debo saber el español para tener un trabajo en las Naciones Unidas?" La mujer le responde "Porque debes hablar dos idiomas para trabajar aquí. Si sabes hablar español puedes trabajar como **diplomática** de **carrera** o como **traductora**". Luego, van al puesto de una **agencia de viajes**. Miguel le pregunta a un señor en el puesto "Estudio español, pero no sé por qué necesito aprender el español". El señor le responde "Bueno, hay muchas **oportunidades** en nuestro **negocio** para las personas que hablan español. Por ejemplo, puedes ser **guía de turismo.** También puedes trabajar en nuestras oficinas como **agente de viajes**. Aprende bien el español y al terminar el año puedes **solicitar** un trabajo en nuestras oficinas".

Al día siguiente Claudia y sus amigos van a la clase de español muy felices. Todos hablan de porque es importante saber el español. El Sr. Gómez está muy contento y dice "¡Es un **milagro**! ¿Qué pasa chicos?" Claudia le dice "¡Quiero ser diplomática en España!" José grita "¡Quiero ser agente de viajes!" La clase está hablando muy alto. El Sr. Gómez grita "¡Silencio! ¡Felicitaciones! ¡Entonces, tenemos que aprender más español!"

Purpose: To use the vocabulary to tell a story.

1. Display the vocabulary list (page 73) in class. Students use the list as a reference.

2. Show illustrations (page 75), then tell the story. Have students follow along.

3. Pick student actors for the story.

4. Tell the story in an animated way. At the same time help student actors perform the story.

5. Ask **Yes/No Questions**.

¿Van Claudia y sus amigos a un restaurante? (no)
¿Van ellos primero al puesto de las Naciones Unidas? (sí)
¿Van ellos luego a la clase de matemáticas? (no)
¿Pueden ellos solicitar un trabajo en la agencia de viajes al terminar el año? (sí)
¿Está triste con sus estudiantes el Sr. Gómez? (no)

6. Ask **Comprehension Questions** about the story.

¿Por qué dice el Sr. Gómez que Claudia y sus amigos tienen que ir a la feria de trabajo?	Para que ellos puedan aprender porque el español es importante en el mundo.
¿A qué puesto van ellos primero?	Ellos van al puesto de las Naciones Unidas.
¿En qué puede trabajar Claudia en las Naciones Unidas?	Puede trabajar como diplomática de carrera o como traductora.
¿A qué puesto van ellos después?	Van al puesto de una agencia de viajes.
¿Qué quiere ser José?	José quiere ser agente de viajes.

7. Read the **Changed Story** and have students correct it.

Claudia y sus amigos están en la clase de español y le gritan al Sr. Gómez, su profesor de español, "El español es muy (1) <u>triste</u>. ¿Por qué es tan importante estudiar español?" El Sr. Gómez les responde "Porque va a ser muy importante para su futuro. Esta semana hay una feria de trabajo en el gimnasio. Como tarea ustedes tienen que ir a esa feria y aprender por qué el español es importante en el mundo".

Después del colegio, Claudia y sus amigos van a la feria de trabajo. Primero, van (2) <u>al caballo</u> de las Naciones Unidas. Claudia le pregunta a una mujer que está en el puesto "¿Por qué debo saber el español para tener un trabajo en (3) <u>los Estados Unidos</u>?" La mujer le responde "Porque debes hablar dos idiomas para trabajar aquí. Si sabes hablar español puedes trabajar como diplomática de carrera o como traductora". Luego, van al puesto de una agencia de viajes. Miguel le pregunta a un señor en el puesto "Estudio español, pero no sé por qué necesito aprender el español". El señor le responde "Bueno, hay muchas oportunidades en nuestro negocio para las personas que hablan español. Por ejemplo, puedes ser (4) <u>basquetbolista.</u> También puedes trabajar en nuestras oficinas como agente de viajes. Aprende bien el español y al terminar el año puedes solicitar un trabajo en nuestras oficinas".

Al día siguiente Claudia y sus amigos van a la clase de español muy felices. Todos hablan de porque es importante saber el español. El Sr. Gómez está muy contento y dice "¡Es (5) <u>muy largo</u>! ¿Qué pasa chicos?" Claudia le dice "¡Quiero ser diplomática en España!" José grita "¡Quiero ser agente de viajes!" La clase está hablando muy alto. El Sr. Gómez grita "¡Silencio! ¡Felicitaciones! ¡Entonces, tenemos que aprender más español!"

Answer Key:
(1) trabajoso (2) al puesto (3) las Naciones Unidas (4) guía de turismo (5) un milagro

8. Collaborate with students in establishing a list of guide words. **Note:** Guide words are a brief list of difficult words or phrases that occur in the story. Display the guide words.

9. Have students practice with partners using only the story's illustrations (page 75) and the guide words (if needed).

10. Have volunteers tell the story to the class. Students may use illustrations and guide words, if necessary.

11. Assessment: Have students record the story on audiocassettes. Students may use **only** the illustrations. Guide words may be used by students who need more direction. Evaluate the cassettes and include them in students' portfolios.

12. Collaborate with students in writing the story based on the illustrations. Write the story as students copy it.

13. Have partners invent a new story or alter the original story. Have them draw new or altered illustrations and then tell the story to the class.

CAPÍTULO 10

Step 1 | Gesturing New Vocabulary

Purpose: To introduce the new vocabulary.

1. Show the vocabulary list on the right, covering up the English and Gesture columns.
2. Introduce the first three words/ expressions.
3. Say the words one at a time and do the gestures.
4. Have students imitate the gestures silently.
5. Say the words and have students gesture with their eyes closed.
6. Test individual students randomly. Say a word and have students do the gesture. (If a word is not understood by several students, it must be included when teaching the following set of words.)
7. Do gestures and have students say the words.
8. Say the words and have students give the English equivalents.
9. Repeat this process (Steps 1-8) for the next set of three words until the vocabulary list is all presented.
10. Ask questions and have students answer.

   Sample Questions:
   ¿Cuáles son algunas cosas que necesitamos proteger?
   ¿Te gusta observar las aves?
   ¿Qué cosas te entusiasman?
   ¿Qué sabes de las selvas tropicales?
   ¿Planeas para el futuro? ¿Cómo?

11. The following day review the vocabulary list using the above steps with increased speed.
12. You may also want to check students' comprehension by creating matching quizzes and fill-in-the-blank exercises.

Note: Some ways to invent gestures include referencing American Sign Language books, making them up or soliciting student input.

Spanish	English	Gesture
(ellos) lo contratan	(they) hire him	Pretend to sign a contract as you gesture to a male student and pretend to saw wood.
planear	to plan	Point to a map and take notes.
entusiasmado	enthusiastic	Act enthusiastic.
(ellos) vuelan	(they) fly	Make a flying motion.
(él/ella) bucea	(he/she) scuba dive	Pretend to scuba dive.
el arrecife de coral	coral reef	Draw coral branches with fish on the blackboard.
clara	clear	Hold up a glass of water.
tibia	warm	Point to 70 degrees on a thermometer.
vivos	bright	Show bright colors.
magnífica	magnificent	Show thumbs up.
las selvas tropicales	rain forest	Draw a jungle with birds on the blackboard.
observar	to watch	Pretend to look at something using binoculars.
las aves	birds	Point to birds.
el pueblo	town	Say the name of a town.
aislados	isolated	Isolate two students and point to them.
el arqueólogo	archeologist	Hammer a rock.
proteger	to protect	Have a student stand behind you and hold up your palms toward the class.

Additional Vocabulary
(él) se empeña, final, peces, no tengan (Uds.), (nosotros) estábamos

Situations

1. Josefina y Amalia **vuelan** a Yucatán para ir al mundo maya. Van a estar allí por dos semanas. Ellas están muy **entusiasmadas**. Cuando las chicas llegan allí, Josefina le pregunta a Amalia "¿Qué quieres hacer primero?" Amalia le responde "Primero quiero **bucear** y ver **el arrecife de coral**. ¿Y tú?" "Pues, yo quiero ir a **las selvas tropicales**." Josefina va en autobús a las selvas tropicales y Amalia camina a la playa para ir a bucear.

2. Josefina **observa las aves** en las selvas tropicales. Ella mira todo tipo de aves **magníficas** con sus binoculares. Ella camina y camina y mira las aves, pero no mira por dónde camina. De repente, ella se tropieza con una roca y se cae. Un tigre sale de los árboles y Josefina grita "¡Auxilio, auxilio!" Josefina piensa "Nadie me oye porque estoy muy **aislada. El pueblo** más cerca está a diez millas de aquí. ¿Qué voy a hacer?" De repente, un **arqueólogo** llega y le dice "No tengas miedo. Yo te voy a **proteger**". Él le da al tigre una hamburguesa y, luego, corren rápidamente. Ella le da un abrazo a él. Él lleva a Josefina a su hotel.

3. Amalia está muy nerviosa porque Josefina no llega. Amalia **planea contratar** a algunos hombres para ir a buscarla en las selvas tropicales. De repente, el arqueólogo llega al hotel con Josefina en sus brazos. Amalia le dice "Muchas gracias, señor". Él le responde "De nada. Con gusto". Amalia le pregunta a Josefina "¿Estás bien?" Josefina le responde "Sí, muy bien. ¿Cómo estuvo el arrecife de coral?" Amalia le dice "Estuvo excelente. Es muy bonito. El agua es muy **clara** y **tibia**. Debes ir. Los peces son muy bonitos y tienen colores muy **vivos**". "Qué bien que tuviste un buen día. Bueno, son las nueve y media. Vamos a comer. Tengo mucha hambre."

Advanced Story

Un viaje al mundo maya

José recuerda lo que el agente de viajes le dijo durante la feria de trabajo. Él se empeña en estudiar mucho para aprender muy bien el español y así poder solicitar el trabajo en la agencia de viajes. Al final del año, José va a la agencia de viajes a solicitar un trabajo y ellos lo **contratan**. Su primer trabajo en la agencia es **planear** un viaje al mundo maya para un grupo de quince personas.

Después de un mes de planear el viaje, todo está listo. El grupo está muy **entusiasmado**. Ellos **vuelan** en Mayan World Airlines a Yucatán, México. Allí, el grupo **bucea** en un **arrecife de coral**. El agua es muy **clara** y **tibia**. Ven muchos tipos de peces de colores muy **vivos.** A todo el grupo le gusta mucho esta **magnífica** experiencia. Luego, el grupo va a **las selvas tropicales** para **observar las aves**. Las aves hacen mucho ruido. De repente, José oye "Sssssssss". Mira a un árbol y ve una cobra muy grande. José le grita al grupo "¡No tengan miedo y corran rápidamente!" Todos corren al **pueblo** y le dicen a José "Eres nuestro héroe. En la selva estábamos muy **aislados** de la civilización". El grupo regresa a los Estados Unidos muy contento. Al final de esta experiencia José decide ser **arqueólogo** para ayudar a **proteger** el mundo maya.

Purpose: To use the vocabulary to tell a story.

1. Display the vocabulary list (page 77) in class. Students use the list as a reference.

2. Show illustrations (page 79), then tell the story. Have students follow along.

3. Pick student actors for the story.

4. Tell the story in an animated way. At the same time help student actors perform the story.

5. Ask **Yes/No Questions**.

   ¿Contrata la agencia de viajes a José? (sí)
   ¿Vuelan ellos a los Estados Unidos? (no)
   ¿Ve el grupo peces de colores muy vivos? (sí)
   ¿Hacen las aves poco ruido? (no)
   ¿Estuvo el grupo muy aislado de la civilización? (sí)

6. Ask **Comprehension Questions** about the story.

¿Qué recuerda José?	Él recuerda lo que el agente de viajes le dijo durante la feria de trabajo.
¿Qué hace el grupo en el arrecife de coral?	Ellos bucean.
¿Qué hace el grupo en las selvas tropicales?	Ellos observan las aves.
¿Por qué corre el grupo al pueblo?	Porque hay una cobra en un árbol.
¿Qué decide ser José después del viaje?	Decide ser un arqueólogo.

7. Read the **Changed Story** and have students correct it.

   José recuerda lo que el agente de viajes le dijo durante la feria de trabajo. Él se empeña en estudiar mucho para aprender muy bien el español y así poder solicitar el trabajo en la agencias de viajes. Al final del año, José va a la agencia de viajes a solicitar un trabajo y ellos lo (1) <u>comprenden</u>. Su primer trabajo en la agencia es (2) <u>escribir</u> un viaje al mundo maya para un grupo de quince personas.

   Después de un mes de planear el viaje, todo está listo. El grupo está muy entusiasmado. Ellos vuelan en Mayan World Airlines a Yucatán, México. Allí, el grupo (3) <u>juega</u> en un arrecife de coral. El agua es muy clara y tibia. Ven muchos tipos de peces de colores muy vivos. A todo el grupo le gusta mucho esta magnífica experiencia. Luego, el grupo va a las selvas tropicales para (4) <u>cocinar</u> las aves. Las aves hacen mucho ruido. De repente, José oye "Sssssssss". Mira a un árbol y ve una cobra muy grande. José le grita al grupo "¡No tengan miedo y corran rápidamente!" Todos corren al pueblo y le dicen a José "Eres nuestro héroe. En la selva estábamos muy (5) <u>contentos</u> de la civilización". El grupo regresa a los Estados Unidos muy contento. Al final de esta experiencia José decide ser arqueólogo para ayudar a proteger el mundo maya.

   Answer Key:
   (1) contratan (2) planear (3) bucea (4) observar (5) aislados

8. Collaborate with students in establishing a list of guide words. **Note:** Guide words are a brief list of difficult words or phrases that occur in the story. Display the guide words.

9. Have students practice with partners using only the story's illustrations (page 79) and the guide words (if needed).

10. Have volunteers tell the story to the class. Students may use illustrations and guide words, if necessary.

11. Assessment: Have students record the story on audiocassettes. Students may use **only** the illustrations. Guide words may be used by students who need more direction. Evaluate the cassettes and include them in students' portfolios.

12. Collaborate with students in writing the story based on the illustrations. Write the story as students copy it.

13. Have partners invent a new story or alter the original story. Have them draw new or altered illustrations and then tell the story to the class.

Appendix

High-frequency TPR Vocabulary

Spanish	English	Gesture
¡Abraza...!	Hug...!	Pretend to give someone a big hug.
¡Abre...!	Open...!	Pretend to open a door.
¡Agarra...!	Get...!	Grab an imaginary object.
¡Apaga...!	Turn off...!	Turn off an imaginary light switch.
¡Aplaude!	Clap!	Applaud.
¡Atrapa...!	Catch...!	Pretend to catch an invisible object.
¡Baila!	Dance!	Dance.
¡Bebe!	Drink!	Pretend to drink from a glass.
¡Besa...!	Kiss...!	Pucker lips and make kissing noises.
¡Busca...!	Look for...!	Look through an imaginary magnifying glass.
¡Camina!	Walk!	Walk.
¡Canta!	Sing!	Sing "la, la, la...."
¡Carga...!	Carry...!	Carry something.
¡Cierra...!	Close...!	Pretend to close a door.
¡Come!	Eat!	Grab imaginary food, put it in mouth and chew.
¡Corre!	Run!	Run in place.
¡Corta!	Cut!	Make scissors with your hand and cut the air.
¡Dale...!	Give him/her...!	With palm facing up, reach out and give a pretend object to somebody.
¡Date la vuelta!	Turn around!	Turn around.
¡Dibuja...!	Draw...!	Hold an imaginary pencil and draw in the air.
¡Enciende...!	Turn on...!	Turn on an imaginary light switch.
¡Escribe!	Write!	Pretend to trace words in the air.
¡Estornuda!	Sneeze!	Sneeze.
¡Grita!	Yell!	Yell.
¡Levántate!	Get up!	Stand up.
¡Llama (a la puerta)!	Knock (on the door)!	Pretend to knock on a door.
¡Llora!	Cry!	Rub eyes and cry.
¡Mira...!	Look at...!/Watch...!	Point to eye and then move finger away as eyes follow it.
¡Para!	Stop!	Put hand out in front of body with palm facing out.
¡Pinta...!	Paint...!	Hold an imaginary paint brush and paint in the air.
¡Pregunta...!	Ask...!	Trace a question mark in the air and shrug shoulders.
¡Recoge...!	Pick up...!	Drop an imaginary object and then pick it up.
¡Ríe!	Laugh!	Laugh.
¡Saca...!	Take out...!	Pretend to take out an object from a box.
¡Salta!	Jump!	Jump.
¡Señala...!	Point to...!	Point to different objects in the room.
¡Siéntate!	Sit down!	Sit down.
¡Silba!	Whistle!	Whistle.
¡Susurra!	Whisper!	Whisper.
¡Tira...!	Throw...!	Pretend to throw an invisible object.
¡Toca...!	Touch...!	Touch an object.
¡Toma...!	Take...!	With right hand, grab an imaginary object from left hand.
¡Tose!	Cough!	Cough into your hand.
¡Ve...!	Go...!	Walk to another part of the classroom.

Adverbs

Spanish	English	Gesture
en voz alta	loudly	Say something in a loud voice.
en voz baja	softly	Say something in a low voice.
lentamente	slowly	Sit down slowly.
rápidamente	fast	Sit down quickly.

Adjectivies

Spanish	English	Gesture
grande	big	Point to something big.
pequeño/a	little	Point to something small.

El cuerpo

la boca	mouth	*la garganta*	throat
el brazo	arm	*el hombro*	shoulder
la cabeza	head	*la mano*	hand
la cadera	hip	*el nariz*	nose
la cara	face	*el ombligo*	belly button
el codo	elbow	*el ojo*	eye
el cuello	neck	*la oreja*	ear
el cuerpo	body	*el pelo*	hair
el dedo	finger	*el pie*	foot
la espalda	back	*la pierna*	leg
el estómago	stomach	*la rodilla*	knee
la frente	forehead	*el dedo del pie*	toe

Los colores

amarillo	yellow	*morado*	purple
anaranjado	orange	*negro*	black
azul	blue	*rosado*	pink
blanco	white	*rojo*	red
café	brown	*verde*	green
gris	gray		

La clase

la banda elástica	rubber band	*la página*	page
el bolígrafo	pen	*la pared*	wall
el borrador	eraser	*la perforadora*	hole punch
la calculadora	calculator	*el periódico*	newspaper
el cesto de papeles	wastebasket	*la pizarra*	(chalk)board
el/la chico/a	boy/girl	*el/la profesor(a)*	teacher
el chinche	thumbtack	*el proyector*	overhead projector
la cinta	tape	*la puerta*	door
la clase	class	*el pupitre*	pupil's desk
el clip	paper clip	*la regla*	ruler
la computadora	computer	*el reloj*	clock, watch
el cuaderno	notebook	*la revista*	magazine
el engrapador	stapler	*el sacapuntas*	pencil sharpener
el escritorio	desk	*la silla*	chair
el/la estudiante	student	*el suelo*	floor
la hoja de papel	sheet of paper	*el tablero de anuncios*	bulletin board
el lápiz	pencil	*el televisor*	television
el libro	book	*las tijeras*	scissors
la luz	light	*la tiza*	chalk
el mapa	map	*el techo*	ceiling
el marcador	marker	*la ventana*	window
la mochila	backpack	*la videocasetera*	VCR

Sample TPR Lesson

The Sample TPR Lesson gives a step-by-step model that shows how words in the High-frequency TPR Vocabulary (page 81) can be taught to students. It consists of selected words and expressions from this vocabulary list, steps to follow in teaching them, a narrative in which these words are used in context and several extension activities. Teachers may want to use this lesson before they start teaching the Basic and Advanced Stories in this manual. Another option is to use this lesson as the first in a series of lessons to teach all or part of the High-frequency TPR Vocabulary.

Vocabulary

Spanish	English
(ella) busca	(she) looks for
el lápiz	pencil
la hoja de papel	sheet of paper
la mochila	backpack
(ella) llora	(she) cries
en voz alta	loudly
(él) se levanta	(he) gets up
rápidamente	fast
(él) camina	(he) walks
(él) le da	(he) gives
(ella) abraza	(she) hugs
(él) se sienta	(he) sits down
el pupitre	pupil's desk

Step 1: Give three commands and gesture them. Students follow silently as they associate the gestures with the vocabulary.

Teacher says: *¡Busca un lápiz! ¡Busca una hoja de papel! ¡Busca una mochila!*

Step 2: Give the same three commands in a different order. Have students gesture them and then gesture them yourself.

Teacher says: *¡Busca una mochila! ¡Busca un lápiz! ¡Busca una hoja de papel!*

Step 3: Give the same three commands in a different order. Have students gesture them.

Teacher says: *¡Busca una hoja de papel! ¡Busca una mochila! ¡Busca un lápiz!*

Step 4: Give one command and gesture another. (This indicates whether or not students understand the words or need more practice.)

Teacher says: *¡Busca una mochila!*
Teacher models: *¡Busca un lápiz!*

Step 5: Continue to teach the three commands by repeating Steps 1-4.

Step 6: Give three new commands consecutively. Have students gesture all three of them in the correct order. (Give three sets of these commands.)

Teacher says: *¡Camina rápidamente! ¡Siéntate! ¡Levántate!*
¡Abraza! ¡Llora en voz alta! ¡Busca un lápiz!
¡Dame un lápiz! ¡Dame tu mochila! ¡Dame una hoja de papel!

Step 7: Have students close their eyes. Give commands in groups of three and have students gesture them. Check comprehension and reteach any gestures that students are not performing reliably. Check students' comprehension individually.

Step 8: Give commands and have students gesture them silently. Combine vocabulary in a unique and humorous way.

Teacher says: *¡Camina rápidamente hacia* (name of student)*!*
¡Abraza tu mochila!
¡Siéntate en una hoja de papel!

Continue to give commands by combining the words and expressions on the vocabulary list. Check students' understanding.

Step 9: Tell the following story in an animated way. At the same time help students act it out. To give students a visual clue to help them remember the story, place people and objects consistently in specific places in the classroom.

Teacher says: *Isabel y Pedro están en la clase. Isabel **busca** un **lápiz** y una **hoja de papel**. Ella busca y busca en su **mochila** pero sólo hay una regla. Ella **llora en voz alta**. Pedro **se levanta rápidamente** y **camina** hacia Isabel. Él **le da** a Isabel un lápiz. Ella **abraza** a Pedro. Pedro **se sienta** en su **pupitre**.*

Step 10: Do extension activities for variety. Play games such as "Bingo" and "Simon Says."

Step 11: Have students make their own dictionary by drawing each new vocabulary word on the list and identifying it in Spanish under the picture.

Basic Story

(él) tiene

Son las nueve y media.

buenos días

(ella) dice

(él) mira

la muchacha

(yo) quiero

hablar

¿Qué hora es?

Son las diez menos veinte.

(él) escribe

¡Hasta mañana!/¡Hasta luego!

me llamo

¿Cómo te llamas?

Mucho gusto.

¿Cuántos años tienes?

Tengo catorce años.

¿De dónde eres?

Soy de Guatemala.

Gracias.

de nada

Advanced Story

de la mañana

(ella) escucha

¿Cómo estás?

Estoy muy mal.

¿Por qué?

(ella) pregunta

Me duele la cabeza.

Lo siento.

¡Adiós!

la boca

Estoy regular.

Estás muy bien.

el catarro

Me duele el estómago.

perdón

(él) corre

los brazos

¿Cómo está usted?

(ella) se tropieza

(ella) está tarde

Basic Story

(ella) está muy nerviosa

piensa

estudiar

(ella) necesita

por teléfono

No sé.

el número

(ella) llama

hay

la impresora láser

Te veo aquí (mañana).

(ella) va

allí

nueva

rápida

terminar

el correo electrónico

mi amiga

el poema de amor

Advanced Story

la mochila

roja

amarilla

caramba

pesada

la revista

el papel

los lápices

los bolígrafos

las reglas

los borradores

las chicas

los chicos

los libros

la puerta

Basic Story

en avión

(ellas) llegan

(ellas) toman un autobús

a pie

cerca de

(ellas) comen

la ensalada

el pescado

solamente

(ellas) toman agua

le duele

el estómago

el baño

la policía

lejos de

la biblioteca

(ella) grita

¡Claro!

la médica

el agua de la llave

Advanced Story

la taquería

el jugo de naranja

Tanto gusto.

Encantado.

simpática

pues

el mesero

el arroz con pollo

los frijoles negros

siempre

pero

la comida

caminar

bueno

(él) besa

la mano

es que

en metro

Basic Story

(ellos) piden

(ellos) van de compras

el padre

nada

la madre

amable

(ellas) juegan

el tenis

el béisbol

atlético

divertido

(yo) tengo que

la tarea

(ella) oye

la radio

difícil

después de

cómico

(él) le da

generoso

Advanced Story

la hermana menor

las fotos

los abuelos

el abuelo

calvo

la abuela

el tío

la prima

la hija única

el hermano mayor

(él) canta

me gusta

(yo) quiero

delgado

triste

toda

contenta

cariñosa

Basic Story	**Advanced Story**
junio	(ella) hace un viaje
el cumpleaños	la semana
todos	el fútbol
(ellos) vienen	anteayer
la sorpresa	montar
(ella) abre	la pelota
(ellos) entran	rápidamente
la caja	buscar
¡Feliz cumpleaños!	vieja
(él) salta	doscientos
la canción	soñar
tan	el pelo
el disco compacto	los ojos
(tú) puedes	la guitarra
el dinero	quinientas
miles	(ella) llora
todos los días	pasar

Basic Story

el rey

la reina

los invitados

(ellos) ponen la mesa

el comedor

las cucharas

los cuchillos

los tenedores

los platos

las servilletas

los vasos

la cocina

la sopa

la pimienta

(él) corre

los cubiertos

atrapar

quemándose

de prisa

Advanced Story

(ellos) encienden

las lámparas

el aceite

(ella) empieza

(ellos) viajaron

al lado de

Tengo hambre.

Tengo sed.

esta

especial

por la noche

las salas

la planta baja

los cuartos

el primer piso

las escaleras

¡Ayúdenme!

la piscina

Tengo frío.

Basic Story

espera

Hace buen tiempo.

Hace...grados.

Hace mucho sol.

Está nublado.

el básquetbol

el basquetbolista

¿Qué tiempo hace?

(él) envía

el invierno

Está nevando.

la nieve

esquiar

patinar sobre hielo

el ajedrez

por la noche

los videojuegos

afuera

Advanced Story

la telenovela

el novio

celoso

el pintor

esta noche

el control remoto

el programa

apaga

el televisor

ahora mismo

déjame

llorando

(yo) alquilo

(el apartamento) cuesta

estupendo

dormir

(ella) permite

casi

todavía

Basic Story

cocinar

(ella) aprendió

la receta

(ella) trabaja

la olla

(ella) añade

las cebollas

las zanahorias

los guisantes

el arroz

el chorizo

(ella) prueba

hace falta

(ella) olvida

quemada

tan buena como

mejor

el mundo

(ella) sonríe

Advanced Story

la gente

(yo) admiro

el armario

los quehaceres

(yo) arreglé

(yo) pasé la aspiradora

(yo) saqué la basura

(yo) limpié

el abrigo

(yo) colgué

la ropa

(tú) tocaste

casarte

conmigo

la campana

quizás

Basic Story	Advanced Story
el viaje	el desfile de modas
(ellos) pagan	la blusa
el centro comercial	la seda
los hombres	rosada
los pantalones	la bufanda
el algodón	la falda
la lana	larga
las camisas	el bolso
el traje de baño	los zapatos
los guantes	la corbata
las chaquetas	el sombrero
las mujeres	le queda
las botas	el vestido de novia
el impermeable	la pulsera
la ropa interior	hace juego
en efectivo	los aretes
llevar	el collar
bronceado	las perlas
las gafas de sol	el perfume

Basic Story

trabajoso

el puesto

las Naciones Unidas

la diplomática

la carrera

la traductora

la agencia de viajes

las oportunidades

el negocio

el guía de turismo

el agente de viajes

solicitar

el milagro

Advanced Story

(ellos) lo contratan

planear

entusiasmado

(ellos) vuelan

(él/ella) bucea

el arrecife de coral

clara

tibia

vivos

magnífica

las selvas tropicales

observar

las aves

el pueblo

aislados

el arqueólogo

proteger

Assessment Rubric

To assess their students' participation in TPR Storytelling, teachers may choose first to evaluate how each individual student retells a situation or story. This type of assessment focuses on presentational skills. Teachers may also evaluate how their students perform as part of a group in revising and retelling a situation or story. This type of assessment focuses on interpersonal communication.

Whether teachers focus on the presentational or interpersonal mode, they should share the following criteria with their students before storytelling begins:

> Completion of Task
> Creativity
> Effort and Risk Taking
> Organization
> Pronunciation
> Variety of Expression
> Use of Gestures and/or Props
> Use of Illustrations/Visuals
> Cultural Appropriateness
> Originality
> Accuracy of Language
> Use of Vocabulary

In addition to the criteria listed above, teachers may want to include the criteria used in the *ACTFL Performance Guidelines for K-12 Learners*:

> Comprehensibility (How well are students understood?)
> Comprehension (How well do students understand?)
> Language Control (How accurate is students' language?)
> Vocabulary Use (How extensive and applicable is students' vocabulary?)
> Communication Strategies (How do students maintain communication?)
> Cultural Awareness (How is students' cultural understanding reflected in their communication?)

Creating the Assessment Rubric

To create a personalized assessment rubric, choose any five criteria from the two lists above and enter them on the sample blank rubric on the following page.

TPR Storytelling

Name: _____

Date: _____

Chapter: _____

Evaluator: _____

Circle one:　　　　Presentational　　　　Interpersonal

For each criterion, rate students from 5 to 0:

　　　　5 = outstanding performance
　　　　4 = good performance
　　　　3 = fair performance
　　　　2 = weak performance
　　　　1 = less than acceptable
　　　　0 = no evidence of participation

Criteria	5	4	3	2	1	0
Total points: _____ x 4 = _____						

Bibliography

Asher, James J. *Learning Another Language Through Actions: The Complete Teacher's Guidebook.* 5th ed. Los Gatos, CA: Sky Oaks Productions, 1996.

García, Ramiro. *Instructor's Notebook: How to Apply TPR for Best Results.* 2nd ed. Los Gatos, CA: Sky Oaks Productions, 1988.

Krashen, Stephen D. *Writing: Research, Theory and Applications.* Torrance, CA: Laredo Publishing Company, 1984.

Krashen, Stephen D. *The Input Hypothesis: Issues and Implications.* Torrance, CA: Laredo Publishing Company, 1985.

Krashen, Stephen D. *The Power of Reading.* Englewood, CO: Libraries Unlimited, 1993.

Ray, Blaine and Contee Seely. *Fluency through TPR Storytelling.* Berkeley, CA: Command Performance Language Institute, 1998.

Seely, Contee and Elizabeth Romijn. *TPR is More Than Commands — At All Levels.* Berkeley, CA: Command Performance Language Institute, 1995.